The Maine Coast

text and photography by George Wuerthner

American Geographic Publishing

Helena, Montana

ISBN 0-938314-62-9

© 1989 American Geographic Publishing

P.O. Box 5630, Helena, MT 59604. (406) 443-2842
William A. Cordingley, Chairman
Rick Graetz, Publisher
Mark Thompson, Director of Publications
Barbara Fifer, Production Manager

Text and photos (except where otherwise credited)
© 1989 George Wuerthner

Design by Linda McCray

Printed in Korea by Dong-A Printing through Codra
Enterprises, Torrance, California

Left: In Bar Harbor.
Far left: At Stonington.
Top: Echo Lake on Mount Desert Island, Acadia National Park.
Facing page: At Islesford on Little Cranberry Island.
Title page: Sunset at Bass Harbor, Mount Desert Island.

DEDICATION

To my wife and best friend, Mollie Matteson.

ACKNOWLEDGMENTS

` Many people helped increased my knowledge of the Maine coast or assisted in some way with this project. In particular I would like to thank Hank Tyers of the Maine Critical Areas Program, the staff of the College of the Atlantic in Bar Harbor, Robert Lewis of the Maine Department of Marine Resources and Jim Dow at the Maine Nature Conservancy. I also owe a special thanks to Ruthie Matteson of Brunswick, Maine.

ABOUT THE AUTHOR

Photographer-writer George Wuerthner has written six previous books, five published by American Geographic, including *Oregon Mountain Ranges, Idaho Mountain Ranges, Alaska Mountain Ranges, The Adirondacks: Forever Wild,* and co-authored with Mollie Matteson *Vermont: A Portrait of the Land and Its People.* His photography and writings also have appeared in many national publications.

He worked as a botanist, university instructor, high school teacher, wilderness ranger and surveyor.

He makes his home in Livingston, Montana just north of Yellowstone National Park.

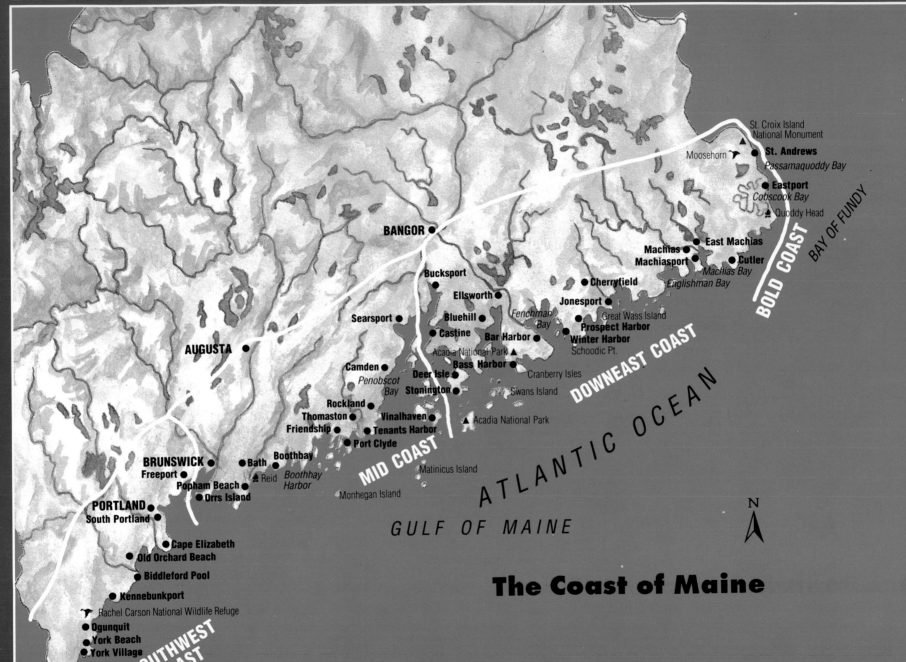

LINDA COLLINS

The Coast of Maine

St. Croix Island
National Monument

Moosehorn
St. Andrews
Passamaquoddy Bay

Eastport
Cobscook Bay

Quoddy Head

BAY OF FUNDY

BOLD COAST

BANGOR

East Machias
Machias
Machiasport
Cutler
Machias Bay
Englishman Bay

Bucksport

Cherryfield

Ellsworth
Jonesport

Fenchman Bay
Great Wass Island

Searsport
Bluehill
Prospect Harbor
Castine
Winter Harbor
Bar Harbor
Schoodic Pt.

Acadia National Park ▲

DOWNEAST COAST

AUGUSTA

Camden
Bass Harbor
Penobscot Bay
Deer Isle
Cranberry Isles
Stonington
Swans Island

Rockland
Vinalhaven
Thomaston
▲ Acadia National Park
Friendship
Tenants Harbor
Port Clyde

ATLANTIC OCEAN

MID COAST

Boothbay
BRUNSWICK
Bath
Matinicus Island
Freeport
Boothbay
Harbor
Reid
Popham Beach
Monhegan Island
Orrs Island

PORTLAND
South Portland

GULF OF MAINE

N

Cape Elizabeth
Old Orchard Beach

Biddleford Pool

Kennebunkport

Rachel Carson National Wildlife Refuge

Ogunquit
York Beach
York Village

SOUTHWEST COAST

Kittery

CONTENTS

*I*ntroduction

Facing page: Portland Head Lighthouse is fewer than 10 miles from Maine's largest urban area, Portland. Quality-of-life factors such as the magnificent coastal landscape increasingly have fueled the Maine coastal economy. According to state economist Charles Colgan, the parts of Maine that have seen the greatest population and employment increases share one common denominator, "they tend to be regions that offer beautiful scenery."

I have visited many shores of this country, but the Maine coast, more than any other, seems to embrace rather than merely border the sea. While most of this nation's coastlines are either straight-edged or drawn with graceful curving lines, the ragged Maine coast looks ripped apart. Actually, it represents what geologists call a "drowned" coast, where a rising sea inundated former river valleys and, in some cases, the coast actually sank.

If you trace every crook and bend of Maine's shore, you find it totals more than 2,400 miles—a more extensive coastline than all the rest of the Eastern Seaboard states combined! Yet, only 228 air miles separate Kittery on the New Hampshire border from Eastport near New Brunswick, Canada. And this shoreline total excludes those of Maine's more than 3,000 offshore islands, which would add another 1,500 miles.

Yet I have driven down numerous long, narrow peninsulas and not known if I were a hundred miles or a hundred feet from the ocean. Dense timber covers all but the most exposed and rugged headlands and islands, obscuring ocean views. It takes faith to keep driving through such a corridor of trees, mile after mile, with no glimmer of the sea in sight, even though the highway map shows you are following some estuary or bay. I always arrive quite suddenly, it seems, at a headland or village next to the sea and find the maps were right after all.

The watery body I am viewing when I finally arrive at the ocean's edge is the Gulf of Maine. It runs from the tip of Cape Cod in Massachusetts northeast to Cape Sable on the southern coast of Nova Scotia, Canada. Very shallow offshore banks such as Georges Bank and Browns Bank restrict circulation between the North Atlantic and Maine's gulf. Between these two banks runs the narrow, but deeper, Northeast Channel.

Water circulates counterclockwise within the Gulf of Maine. After entering the Gulf by Cape Sable on the southern coast of Nova Scotia, the water flows around the upper part of the Bay of Fundy. Then it turns southwest following the New Brunswick shore and Maine coast until deflected eastward near Cape Cod, where the current turns north again. Following Georges Bank, part of the current flows into the North Atlantic, while the rest returns toward the Bay of Fundy for another pass. It takes about three months for gulf waters to make this full circuit.

Because the Gulf of Maine is nearly closed off from the North Atlantic and other currents, it has been called an ocean within a ocean. Particularly vulnerable to any form of pollution, the gulf does not readily expel contaminants. This fact was used to oppose construction of oil refineries here—a recurring proposal—since any oil spills would prove disastrous to coastal marine life.

Limited circulation also gives the Gulf of Maine slightly different chemical and temperature qualities from the North Atlantic. For example, large tides in the Bay of Fundy continuously drag cold water from the bottom of the bay to the surface. Surface temperatures seldom rise above 50°. The temperature difference between shore and water results in numerous foggy days; Washington County, near the mouth of Fundy Bay, boasts the most foggy days in Maine. However, the water in the southern part of the gulf, with smaller

In the Gulf of Maine, which is nearly closed off from the Atlantic Ocean, water takes about three months to make a counter-clockwise circuit.

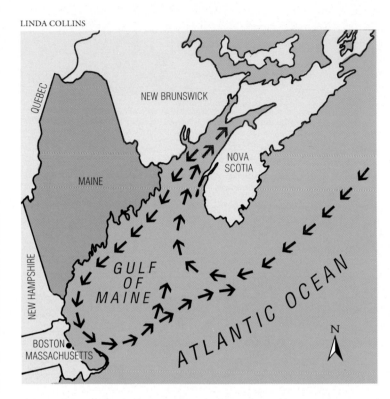

tides, frequently warms to 60° or more, contributing to beachgoers' affection for Southwest Coast resort areas like Old Orchard Beach.

During the summer, southwest winds dominate the Maine coast. They drive surface water offshore, which in turn pulls colder waters upward. Upwelling also results from giant eddies in the gulf. In addition, shallow shelves like Georges Bank push deep currents upward and send nutrients to the surface. This continuous enrichment of the Gulf of Maine accounts for its particularly rich and justifiably famous fisheries.

Not coincidentally, the Maine coast first attracted exploitation by fishermen, not loggers or farmers. Its numerous harbors, rich waters, favorable currents and underwater topography all contributed to making the Gulf of Maine one of the premier fishing "holes" in the nation.

Easy transport also shaped early settlement patterns. Before modern transportation, nearly all travel to and from Maine was by boat and, as a consequence, nearly all human settlement hugged the shore. Even today, the link between communities and the sea is still very evident. Except for a few large cities like Portland, most people still live in small villages along protected nooks or coves and the Maine coast remains largely rural—at least when compared to the rest of New England.

The region comprises only 12 percent of the state's land area, although some of Maine's larger communities are here, including Portland. The southwest coast is the most densely populated coastal area, while the easternmost shores, particularly Washington County, front the state's least-inhabited sections.

Fish exports sustained the coastal economy in the 17th century. In addition, timber harvest of the large white pine, particularly common along Maine's southwest coast, became an important secondary export. During the 1800s, industrialization harnessed numerous waterfalls along coastal rivers for power production, and manufacturers concentrated on textiles, paper, lumber and wood products, and leather. All these industries suffered varying degrees of deterioration after their initial boom periods. Declines in manufacturing, fishing, shipping, logging and farming affected Maine's other economies and even its population. Between 1880 and 1970, Maine's population grew at an average annual rate of only four tenths of a percent, significantly less than the nationwide average of 1.8 percent.

Population has increased recently in both urban and rural coastal areas, but many coastal villages still have smaller populations than a hundred years ago. The development of trains, highways and planes eliminated much of the marine trade and today only 22,000 people, or 3.6 percent of the state's workers, still hold marine-based jobs. Almost half this number, 10,000 people, work at Bath Iron Works—the state's largest private employer. The fishing industry, although a dominant part of coastal economy, employed only 6,627 people in 1988.

But iron workers at Bath or condominium owners at Wells do not bespeak Maine's coastal mythology. The quaint fishing village with lobster boats at anchor does. The small fishing villages that dot the coast suggest a harmony between human presence and the scenic coastline and make coastal life attractive.

Preservation of traditional fishing villages like Cutler, Friendship, Port Clyde and others is analogous to preservation of farmland in Vermont. They are part of what makes Maine Maine. The mythology of the "undiscovered" fishing village fuels Maine's growing tourism industry and contribute to the coast's increasing population. Most new coastal residents came as tourists, fell in love with the coast, then outbid local fishermen for choice coastal real estate, driving real estate prices higher and, ironically, endangering the very attributes that first drew them.

Still, the coast is an attractive place to live and work, and fishermen certainly don't have sole proprietary rights to it. So the new residents come, and with them comes a need for more people in trade and service industries, which now account for most coastal employment, while manufacturing (including the wood products industry) continues to decline.

Since 1970, the year-round population of Maine's coastal communities has risen nearly 50 percent. In addition, more than 43,000 residences along the coast are reported to be primarily vacation homes.

According to Charles Colgan, state economist, the regions of Maine that have seen the greatest population and employment increases share one common denomina-tor: "they tend to be regions that offer beautiful scenery or other amenities that have attracted both tourists and new residents."

Big-ticket industrial developments such as oil refineries or mills, touted during the 1960s and 1970s as the solution to Maine's economic hardships, failed to fulfill their

Many coastal communities like Camden, seen here, are largely dependent upon tourist trade. And it is easy to see why.

promise. However, a steady growth in small and medium-sized businesses is fueling coastal Maine's economic rc-vival. In the past 10 years, population along the coast has grown by 14 percent and employment has increased 32 percent. Trying to deal with a growing labor shortage, fast food establishments like Burger King and McDonald's now advertise flexible hours and good benefits.

Good economic news, though, often obscures the costs of growth. Since almost no one disputes that scenic beauty is fueling economic prosperity, coastal residents worry that continued unregulated development threatens the goose that laid the golden egg.

Residential development, however, threatens more than just scenery. It increasingly threatens marine-depend-ent industries. Only 10 percent of Maine's thousands of miles of shoreline features deep, shcltcrcd waters suitable for harbors. Increasingly, developments like shopping malls and condominiums encroach upon traditional water-front uses like fish processing plants or fishing boat har-bors. In the past, many waterfront sites were undesirable; pollution was widespread and many harbor areas were run down. With the revitalization of these properties, new de-mands for development are occurring. Several communi-ties, including Portland and Yarmouth, now limit water-front developments that are not marine-dependent.

The tourist industry spawns much of the demand for non-marine development. Tourism now brings an esti-mated 6 million people to the Maine coast annually. Four million people each year visit—some would say overrun—Acadia National Park, the second-highest visitation level of any national park. But tourists keep the cash registers ring-ing—they spent approximately $1 billion during 1986.

The summer crush of tourists strains community landfills and sewage facilities, adds congestion to already-crowded streets and highways. Since tourists don't pay taxes to maintain Maine's infrastructure, local taxpayers, particularly those who do not benefit from tourist dollars, often assume an unfair tax burden.

In spite of the coast's popularity, a surprisingly small amount of shoreline is publicly owned and therefore acces-sible. The only substantial public holdings are Acadia Na-tional Park, plus a few widely scattered state parks and na-tional wildlife refuges. This lack of public lands is not an accident, but somewhat the result of antagonism that Mainers have had towards public ownership since the earli-est days of the state. Further opposition to public owner-

Sunset over Blue Hill Bay. The convoluted Maine coast, including islands, totals more than 4,500 miles in length.

least 1,300 islands, most less than an acre, remain state-owned.

Despite this recent re-assertion of public ownership of coastal lands, Maine still ranks first in the nation in private ownership of land. A recent estimate suggests that only 3.5 percent of the shoreline is publicly owned. This contrasts sharply with western states—like Oregon, where 93.5 percent of the coast is publicly owned.

Private citizens bought nearly all Maine's large public tracts, including Baxter State Park and Acadia National Park, and donated them to the state or federal government over the objections of both citizens and political leaders. Recently, citizens stopped a proposed expansion of Acadia National Park on Mount Desert Island, and opposed the creation of a new "Bold Coast National Park" near Cobscook Bay in Washington County. Although opposed to new national parks, Maine's citizens voted for a $35 million bond issue for public acquisition, but access may be a case of too little too late, considering the skyrocketing cost of coastal real estate.

Rising real estate prices affect more than public access. The cost of coastal housing and property soon may price out many long-time residents and traditional industries like fishing. For example, housing costs in York County grew by 20 percent between 1985 and 1987 and the average three-bedroom house cost $95,000, while the median income was only $15,600. Such figures, combined with lack of public access, will mean that only those with wealth may own land on the state's uniquely beautiful coast.

The Maine coast is changing, in many cases rapidly. How well it adjusts to change remains to be seen, but Maine citizens seem to recognize that development must not eclipse responsible land stewardship. Maine needs to preserve the sea and land, and reaffirm the fundamental connection of humanity to both.

ship has come from large-scale investment interests, frequently from out of state.

During Maine's early years, the state sold coastal real estate, particularly islands, as rapidly as possible to finance its operations and boost its tax base. In 1913, it stopped this practice, but not until 1973 did the legislature pass the Coastal Island Registry Act, which required land owners on islands with four or fewer residential structures to prove the validity of their titles. Most owners showed good titles, but private ownership of some 200 islands remains in doubt. At

Private citizens bought nearly all of Maine's large public tracts of land and donated them to the government.

Sunset at Pemaquid Point. The Gulf of Maine, partially cut off from the North Atlantic by shallow offshore banks, has unique chemical and nutrient qualities that make it one of the richest fishing waters in the world.

CLIMATE ALONG THE COAST

Maine's coastal weather has many faces. The coast may be lost in fingers of fog lacing the pointed spruce on headlands or bashed with volley after volley of waves during a winter storm, or it may bask in the sunshine sparkling on the water on a calm summer day.

Most of the air masses that affect the Maine coast flow from the inland areas to the east, causing long, cold winters and sometimes-hot summers. However, the proximity of the ocean moderates an otherwise continental climate. For example, the ocean's post-winter coolness delays spring, but its summer-acquired warmth prolongs warm weather into the fall.

Annual precipitation varies somewhat with location—villages on the outer coast and islands tend to get slightly more rain than more westerly communities. For example, Portland's annual average is 40.8 inches while Machias and Bar Harbor both receive more than 48 inches annually.

Although precipitation is fairly well distributed throughout the year, averaging three to four inches a month, November usually registers a slight increase, and July and August tend to be the driest months of the year. According to weather records, Mainers can expect significant precipitation six to eight days of each month, and severe drought is exceedingly rare. The abundant precipitation and its even distribution throughout the year assure the growth of lush forests, which cover 86 percent of the coast.

Significant rainfall may occur only about 20 percent of the time, but skies are cloudy or partly cloudy about two thirds of the time. Furthermore, the cloudiest weather occurs in late fall, coinciding with the shortest days of the year, a combination that aggravates depression and bouts of cabin fever among many Maine residents. The winters can seem especially long and oppressive. However, all is forgotten when sunny summer weather rolls around.

Even in summer, though, heavy fog inundates many coastal areas. Fog develops when warm air from the land settles over cooler ocean water. The drop in temperature causes water vapor to condense and fog banks develop. Eastport averages fog one in three days during the summer, while Portland peers through fog only once in every five days.

The coastal zone has a remarkably long frost-free season because the ocean soaks up heat during the summer and releases it well into the fall. Eastport boasts a 174-day frost-free season, followed closely by Brunswick, whose growing season is 163 days. Although farther south, Portland averages only 136 frost-free days.

Maine occupies a weather battle-zone. Air masses from the south fight those driven out of the north and the conflict erupts in rapid and frequent changes in weather. A "normal" month is difficult to characterize.

In summer, most winds are from the southwest. But local sea breezes often develop in the afternoons, blowing cooler air from the sea inland and enhancing the Maine coast as a summer resort. West or northwest winds are more likely in winter, although on occasion winds from the northeast produce the famed "northeasters." These storms, charging inland from the North Atlantic, bring the worst kind of weather—cold laced with plenty of wet—as polar

The link between the sea and human life is still very much in evidence along the Maine coast, where small fishing villages, such as Cutler, seen here, remain viable communities.

Forest by Pretty Marsh in Acadia National Park. When you travel the Maine coast, views of the ocean often are obscured by the dense forest that covers 85 percent of coastal landscape.

maritime air masses circle in from Newfoundland and Labrador. Heavy rain or snow, combined with gale-force winds, chills people to the marrow. On average, two such storms pound the coast in a typical winter, and do most of the significant storm damage on the Maine coast. If they originated in the tropics, we might call them hurricanes. True hurricanes, however, rarely assault Maine: the chance of one occurring here is only seven percent in a given year.

Right: Unlike most of the eastern seaboard, the Maine coast is dominated by a rocky shoreline. It is the interface of wave and rock that gives this region its scenic charm.
Facing page: Eagle Lake on Mount Desert Island. Maine's coastal climate is cool and wet. Much of the Maine coast actually gets five to 10 inches more precipitation per year than soggy Portland, Oregon.

Geology

CHAPTER 2

Above: Basalt dike intruded into the existing granite bedrock at Schoodic Head, Acadia National Park.
Facing page: Contorted schists at Pemaquid Point. The ocean has eroded away softer layers of rock while harder layers remain as ridges, creating the groove seen here.

*N*o feature is more emblematic of Maine than its scenic rock-bound coast. It is unlike any other on the Eastern Seaboard. The deeply indented bays and numerous boulder-rimmed islands directly reflect of Maine's geologic past. Understanding Maine's rock history can lead to greater appreciation of the landscape's special character and beauty.

Quite surprising to some people is the theory that rocks that now make up the coast of Maine did not always belong to North America. Large blocks of the earth's crust, in continual motion, drift slowly about the surface of the earth like immense slabs of ice in a partially frozen river. Jostling about, crashing into each other and breaking apart, these crustal blocks continuously create new configurations—but over millions of years.

This movement of continental rocks over the surface of the earth is explained by the theory of plate tectonics. According to plate theory, the earth resembles an apple with a molten core, a thick zone of solid rock called the mantle—analogous to the white, pulpy part of an apple—that surrounds the core, and a very thin skin ("only" 60 miles thick) called the crust.

The crust, the ocean's floor and the continents' bedrock are broken into a dozen or more pieces, or "plates," that float upon the mantle. Radioactive decay deep in the earth provides a heat source that creates convection currents in the molten rock. The currents raft plates about the globe in a random manner. Plates sometimes collide; the lighter continental plates tend to rise up and over the heavier oceanic plates, which are shoved deep into the mantle.

The buried oceanic plates melt into a substance called magma, the material that rises to the surface to create volcanos. For example, an oceanic plate is now diving under the western edge of South America, driving up the Andes and creating a deep oceanic trench along the continent's edge.

Sometimes two continental plates collide, as is occurring where India meets Asia. Here, neither plate is entirely subducted, or pushed beneath the other. Instead, huge mountains (in this case, the Himalayas) rise.

When crustal plates break apart and pull away from one another, as occurred recently (in geologic terms) when North America separated from Europe, magma rises into the fissures between the plates and spreads out over the surface. Magma, called lava when it reaches the earth's surface, then cools and solidifies into a rock known as basalt. If lava flows occur under the ocean, they create new sea floor. Presently, the North American plate is pulling away from the European plate at a rate of two inches per year, while new oceanic crust is being formed along the Mid-Atlantic Ridge, a seam that separates North America from Europe.

Plate tectonics explains the relatively recent geological history of Maine. Some 390 million years ago, the crustal masses that we recognize today as the seven continents comprised only two very large ones. At that time, North America was joined to Europe and Asia. Plants had just colonized land from the oceans, and as yet there were no dinosaurs.

Gradually, even these two giant crustal blocks joined to form one huge super-continent. The collision of these immense land masses buckled up mountains, crushed rocks along the contact zones and shoved ocean basins deep into

Champlain Mountain, Acadia National Park. Passing glaciers plucked rock from the sides of mountains, leaving angular blocks as evidence.

the earth. By 300 million years ago, this super-continent, called Pangaea, was completely united into a single mass and what is now Maine occupied its center. North America and Europe were located somewhere near the equator. A steamy jungle covered much of the landscape. In swampy deltas, abundant plant life was buried, partially decomposed, and began to form the coal now found throughout the Appalachian Mountains.

By 200 million years ago, or shortly after the appearance of the dinosaurs, these crustal blocks began to separate into their present configuration. North America eventually pulled away from Europe and Africa, while the North Atlantic Ocean formed in between. Evidence for the former connection between continents includes rocks under Boston that once may have belonged to Africa; similarities between fossils and rock layers of the Appalachian Mountains and those of the Caledonides Mountains of Scotland; and the limestone fossils at Thomaston that are similar to fossils found in Europe.

Since the new Atlantic Ocean basin did not appear until Pangaea began to break up, no rocks older than 200 million years rest on the Atlantic sea floor. The youngest rocks lie near the spreading sea-floor fracture, while the oldest now lie farthest from the seam.

One result of this reorganization of continental masses was the welding of former West European and African rocks onto North American rocks. These rocks, recognizable as a distinct grouping geologists call the Avalon belt, now make up much of the coast of Maine as well as parts of Nova Scotia and Newfoundland. The Avalon Belt rocks differ from much older rocks found in the Appalachian Mountains and those that make up parts of interior Maine.

About the time the dinosaurs disappeared, some 65 million years ago, North America had drifted both north and west, nearly to its present location. This general drift continues. Maine brings up the rear of a drifting continent—an area that tends to be rather quiet, geologically speaking. Erosion wore the state's features into a more or less flat plain, with only one small period of uplift about 20 million years ago, which rejuvenated rivers and allowed them to alter the old surface.

GLACIATION

It was on this ancient, relatively flat, erosional landscape that the next significant episode in the coast's geologic history occurred. Approximately 2 million years ago, at the beginning of the Pleistocene epoch, world temperatures dropped—perhaps as much as five degrees. Snow accumulated near each pole and solidified into glaciers that grew large enough to flow outward. Giant continental glaciers eventually covered nearly all of Canada and much of today's northern United States—including the entire area of Maine, which was buried under ice 1.2 miles thick. At its maximum extent some 21,000 years ago, the ice extended southeast to what are now Browns and Georges banks along the edge of the continental shelf.

Glacial ice forms when more snow accumulates than melts each year. Eventually its own weight compacts the snow into ice crystals, and bottom layers become somewhat plastic and ooze outward like cold toothpaste. Rocks and boulders plucked from the ground and bedrock become embedded in the bottom of this ice river, effectively creating a giant rasp that scours the landscape, smoothing hills and deepening valleys it passes over.

Many places along the Maine coast show the effects of this glacial scouring. At Acadia National Park, the ice smoothed the bedrock almost to a polish. Striations, or lines gouged into solid bedrock by glaciers, are common on all the mountains in the park, and are particularly notable on Cadillac Mountain. Other signs of glaciers include erratics, boulders and large rocks carried by glaciers and dropped in new locations.

The prevailing direction of glaciers can be inferred from the shapes of mountains and hills. The glaciers planed many mountains in Maine smooth and round on their north slopes, giving them a whale-back appearance. The south sides of these same mountains are often broken and cliff-like where glaciers plucked rocks out. Many mountains in Acadia National Park, like the Porcupine Islands near Bar Harbor, display this kind of glacial sculpting.

When glaciers flow down existing river valleys, they grind and smooth the sides, leaving steepened slopes. At the same time, they deepen and flatten the valley bottom, creating the U-shaped profiles typical of glaciation. If rising sea levels later flood one of these valleys, we call it a fiord. Somes Sound on Mount Desert Island is one of only two glacial fiords on the Eastern Seaboard (the lower Hudson River valley is the other).

Glaciers act as giant conveyor belts and bulldozers,

Above: On South Bubble, Acadia National Park. This rock, transported by glaciers and deposited in this new location, is known as an erratic.
Left: Sunset from Cadillac Mountain, where bedrock was smoothed by the passage of glacial ice that completely covered what is now the Maine coast during the height of the last Ice Age.

transporting along their margins and terminuses huge quantities of dirt, rocks and other debris, often depositing them in heaps we call moraines. When a glacier melts, it leaves behind its morainal load, often forming large hills of unsorted material. Cape Cod, Martha's Vineyard, Nantucket Island and Long Island all represent the terminal moraines of large continental glaciers, marking the most southerly and easterly advances during the last Ice Age.

Moraines, very common along the Maine coast, consist primarily of well drained gravels and sands and lack deep soils. They often are marked by drought-resistant

Above: Chatter marks on Beehive Mountain, Acadia National Park. Gouging by rocks embedded in the bottom of a glacier leaves these distinctive "tracks" on bedrock.
Right: South Bubble, Acadia. The rounded summits of the Bubbles plus the U-shaped valley between them are all classic examples of glaciation.

plant species like white pine and pitch pine. Blueberry barrens also commonly cover glacial moraines.

The immense weight of vast glaciers depresses the land about one foot for every three feet of ice. At its maximum, glacial ice depressed central Maine about 2,000 feet! In addition, huge quantities of seawater froze into glacial ice, dropping the level of the world's oceans 200 to 300 feet. Land-based glaciers therefore extended far beyond the present shorelines before they encountered seas.

Approximately 18,000 years ago, the continental glaciers began to retreat. The terminus of the ice sheet retreated to the present coastline approximately 13,500 years ago. As they melted, the glaciers left behind huge moraines as well as meltwater-washed sediments. In addition, the

ocean invaded the depressed land, submerging much of coastal Maine and, indeed, covering portions of central Maine as far inland as present-day East Millinocket.

Here and there along the Maine coast, glaciers calved icebergs, as they do now off the coast of Greenland. Mountains such as those on Mount Desert Island and in the Camden Hills were merely small islands surrounded by vast stretches of ocean. Marine sediments are common inland as far as Bingham in the Kennebec Valley and Livermore Falls in the Androscoggin Valley—areas presently 400 hundred feet above sea level. Many of the mud flats utilized as clam beds today hold the fine sediments deposited by melting glaciers thousands of years ago.

By 11,000 years ago, no glacial ice remained in Maine,

and the land, relieved of the great weight, rebounded faster than the meltwater-fed oceans could rise. By 6,000 years ago, many places along the Northeast coast had rebounded to heights greater than at present.

However, sea level still is rising as the earth's climate warms and releases more of the water locked in polar glaciers. In addition, some portions of the Maine coast have begun to sink for reasons as yet undetermined. The area around Eastport is dropping at a rate of three feet per century, a phenomenal rate of subsidence. Rising sea levels combined with sinking coasts have created what geologists refer to as Maine's drowned coast. What we perceive today as narrow, deeply indented bays are actually river valleys flooded by rising sea level.

This continual rise in sea level eventually will transform the Maine coast. Some scientists believe the sea may creep inland as much as 3,000 feet, flooding many coastal villages. Erosion of coastal dunes and land, already aggravated by human disturbance and construction, likely will increase. Biologically productive wetlands, already in short supply along Maine's rockbound coast, may flood faster than new ones emerge. Human construction may even prevent new wetlands from forming. In addition, scientists expect the magnitude of tides in the Bay of Fundy and elsewhere in the Gulf of Maine to change.

Rocky ledges at Otter Point in Acadia National Park.

BEACH FORMATION

Sand beaches are rare in Maine—comprising less than two percent of Maine's irregular shore, or only 78 miles of the 3,500 miles of Maine's coastline. Due to their rarity, the state's few sand beaches are a significant natural resource, made even rarer because only 27 percent (20 miles) are actually open to the public.

Due to the hard bedrock and the relative youth of Maine's coastline, nearly all the sand of the state's beaches comes from glacial deposits. The only exceptions are sands provided by the Kennebec River (Popham and Seawall beaches) and the Saco River (Old Orchard and Hills beaches).

Five processes—waves, tides, winds, storms and currents—build or destroy beaches. Waves are the most important force in beach structure. As a wave approaches shore, its crest continues to rush toward shore as the deeper water drags along the bottom. This difference in speed causes a wave to break. Each wave carries sand up onto the beach and back into the sea as well.

Winter storms create larger waves than summer's do, and their ability to pick up sand is greater. As a result, the profile of a beach changes progressively throughout the year. In winter, the waves wash up higher on the beach, and steepen the beach profile. By contrast, the gentle waves of summer pack less erosive and transportation power, and so beaches become flatter and wider. Storms originating far out at sea provide low swells that can build beaches, while storms from close to the coast usually produce high waves that result in beach erosion.

Tides also influence wave erosion and beach construction. The tidal range determines the overall width and height of a beach.

Winds contribute to beach and dune formation. Winds both control the size of waves breaking on the shore and move the sand grains themselves.

Dunes play an important role in sand beach formation. They protect interior areas—often wetlands—from storm waves, salt spray and wind shear. In addition, they serve as "banks" where sand is "saved" for future beach development. Dunes would not develop without vegetation. The roots of plants like American beachgrass catch loose, drifting sand and help to stabilize its motion. Beachgrass can survive only if it is continuously buried. Trampling by humans, however, kills dune vegetation and eventually destroys the dunes themselves. One of the least-disturbed dune and marsh complexes in the state can be seen at Popham Beach State Park.

Maine's coast exhibits four types of beaches: spit, barrier, fringing and tombolo. A spit beach is anchored to land on one end and free at the other. Spit beaches usually result when waves wash ashore at an angle, setting in motion longshore currents. These currents carry sand toward the tail end of a spit. Salt marshes often develop behind sand spits, as has occurred along the Webhannett River near Wells. Sometimes a spit will eventually become anchored at both ends, creating a barrier beach like Mile Beach at Reid State Park. These wetlands are extremely important as nurseries for many kinds of marine life.

Pocket or fringing beaches usually develop between rocky headlands

Facing page: Sand Beach at Acadia is an example of both a pocket beach and barrier beach. The "pocket" between two headlands provides quiet water where offshore currents drop their sand to create small beaches. In the case of Sand Beach, it also has blocked freshwater drainage creating a marsh, hence also qualifies as a barrier beach.

where they are protected from currents that would otherwise sweep away their sand. Usually small, they almost never develop a dune complex or a salt marsh behind. Instead they rest upon the underlying bedrock of the headland. Crescent Beach at Crescent Beach State Park is a pocket beach.

A land bridge between the mainland and an island or between two islands is called a tombolo. Tombolos form when sand carried by swirling currents settles in the quiet backwater eddies behind islands. Two of the best examples of tombolos on the Maine coast also are easily accessible. The bar connecting Mount Desert Island and Bar Island—from which Bar Harbor gets its name—is a classic tombolo, as is the sandy bridge that connects Wood Island to Hunnewell Beach by Popham Beach State Park.

Beaches are dynamic natural features, continuously changing. They cannot be stablized and efforts to stop erosion—such as building jetties and seawalls—actually accelerate their destruction. Seawalls, for example, reflect wave energy rather than absorbing it as do sandy beaches. This increases the velocity of backwash in waves and ultimately their erosive power. Seawalls also disrupt the seasonal winter-summer cycle of beach formation, and beaches eventually disappear. A seawall built to protect houses near Wells actually increased net erosion of the beaches and destroyed the landward movement of nearby dunes. Construction of houses on dunes also interferes with the natural movement of sand, eventually "starving" some dune systems.

Below: Dunes at Popham Beach State Park. Sand beaches and dune formations are relatively rare on the rocky Maine coast. Popham Beach is one of the least disturbed beach complexes in the entire state.
Facing page: Schists—metamorphic, crystalline rock—at Reid State Park, Georgetown.

Ecology
CHAPTER 3

Birch forest, Acadia National Park. Paper birch, a sun-loving species, often sprouts after fires. This grove near Bar Harbor began after the 1947 Fire, which leveled part of the town and burned a portion of Mount Desert Island.

Geology, climate and, today, human activity, all influence Maine's ecological setting. Although 15 percent of the coastal zone is presently cleared for either urban development or agriculture, fully 85 percent of the land is covered by trees. This reflects the climate, which favors tree growth, and the sparseness of human settlement, more than it reflects any human efforts toward preservation. Nevertheless, the state's abundant coastal forests, like its fish, first attracted Europeans. Even today, some 17 percent of Maine's timber harvest occurs within the coastal realm.

Maine's coastal forests can be broadly divided into two major types—conifers and hardwoods. Many people know conifers as "Christmas trees" or "evergreens." The more common conifer species in Maine include white pine, red, white and black spruce, and balsam fir. Less common, but locally important, are jack pine, pitch pine and tamarack (also known as eastern larch).

The leaves of hardwoods, or deciduous trees, turn brilliant colors in the autumn and then drop with the coming of winter. (Tamarack is the only conifer that drops its needles each autumn.) Common hardwood trees along the Maine coast include sugar and red maple, American beech, paper and yellow birch, aspen and white ash.

Even casual observers note that conifers such as spruce and fir dominate the immediate coastal fringe. Indeed, their pointed silhouettes against the sunset remains one of the distinctive sights of the coastal environment. These conifers mark the southern, outlying extensions of the boreal forest that stretches in a nearly continuous band from Maine across Canada all the way to Alaska.

Conifers, such as the various spruce species, are adapted to survive on sites with poor, thin soils and cool, wet climates. Not surprisingly, they thrive best along the cooler eastern coast from Penobscot Bay to Passamaquoddy Bay, where they comprise some 55 to 60 percent of the commercial forest land. East of Machias Bay, spruce-fir forests dominate both coastal and inland sites. But farther south and west, hardwoods comprise a greater share of the warmer inland sites. South of Penobscot Bay, spruce-fir forests usually inhabit only the most exposed headlands, peninsulas and islands.

Although all spruce species are adapted to cool temperatures and generally nutrient-poor soils, individual differences distinguish species. For example, black spruce best tolerates water saturation of its roots and can grow on extremely poor sites such as bogs and heaths. Red spruce, more shade-tolerant than white spruce, tends to inhabit mature forests, while white spruce forms a thin band along more open areas such as the immediate coastal strand.

Due to drier and warmer conditions west and south of Casco Bay, white pine-hardwood forests replace the spruce-fir association in this region, even on headlands and other exposed sites. White pine, along with pitch pine, tends to colonize sandy, well-drained sites such as glacial moraines. Both species also prefer periodic fires, which tend to eliminate competing hardwood species.

While the pines commonly occupy the sandy, nutrient-deficient soils, hardwoods such as sugar maple, yellow birch

Maple at Eagle Lake, Acadia National Park. Hardwoods, such as maple, are more common along the Southwest coast and gradually are replaced by conifers to the north and east coastline.

and American beech typically thrive in deep, loamy, moist soils. The Southwest and Mid-coast regions sport a mixture of conifers and hardwoods.

Two other hardwoods, paper birch and aspen, are fire-adapted species like the white and pitch pines. They do not tolerate shading and thus usually invade disturbed sites like logged or burned areas. Both species are very common on the eastern side of Mount Desert Island, which burned in 1947. With time, these sun-loving species will give way to more shade-tolerant species, like sugar maple or spruce.

Without periodic disturbances such as fires, insect infestations or even human-caused disturbances like logging, sun-loving species like aspen and paper birch gradually would disappear from the landscape. After disturbance, recolonization by different plant species follows a somewhat predictable sequence called succession, based on each plant's specific tolerances and adaptations.

Paper birch and aspen, both "pioneer" species, adapt best to situations in which the forest canopy has been removed. For example, aspen can resprout from its roots if the aboveground boles are destroyed by logging, fire or other disturbance. Since the young tree can draw upon an existing, well established root system, it grows faster and out-competes other trees like balsam fir, which must germinate from seed and take years to develop root systems.

However, fir tolerates shade much better than aspen. Thus, young balsam firs may establish themselves in the understory of an aspen grove, growing slowly and gradually replacing the fast-growing aspen as it dies. But the fir,

As with tree species, different bird species are adapted and specialized for specific habitats. For example, some 28 species of birds frequent coastal wetlands, including Virginia rail, common gallinule, Wilson's snipe, marsh wren, red-winged blackbird, Wilson's warbler and swamp sparrow.

However, the richest diversity of bird species occurs in forests. The many layers in the forest canopy offer different ecological niches for exploitation, hence greater opportunities for diversification of species dependent upon this ecosystem. For example, the Cape May warbler feeds only in the crown of a spruce, while the bay-breasted warbler exploits the interior branches and the myrtle warbler the lower branches and trunk. In this way all three species can utilize the same habitat without direct competition.

Mature spruce-fir forests typically support the golden-crowned kinglet, hermit thrush, and blackburnian, black-throated green, Cape May, Tennessee and yellow-rumped warblers. In younger forests, parula and magnolia warblers, along with dark-eyed juncos and white-throated sparrows abound.

Deciduous forests shelter other birds, including the red-eyed vireo, ovenbird, least flycatcher, American redstart, wood thrush, ruffed grouse and yellow-bellied sapsucker. Mature hardwoods occasionally host the pileated woodpecker, scarlet tanager and rose-breasted grosbeak.

Due to Maine's brief summer, most nesting occurs in mid-May through early June, with a delay of as much as 10 days between the cooler Downeast coastal regions and the warmer Southwest coast.

like most other shade-tolerant trees, merely survives, making the best of a poor situation. When an opening in the canopy does occur, suppressed trees grow rapidly.

TERRESTRIAL WILDLIFE

The wildlife found in Maine's coastal terrestrial environments does not differ substantially from wildlife found in the rest of Maine. Hence, generalizations about the state apply to the coastal environment as well. Birds are probably one of the most conspicuous dwellers of the forest and shore. More than 230 species of terrestrial birds have been recorded in Maine; however, only about 170 can be considered relatively common. And as might be expected in such a cold climate, a very small number, 50 or so species, reside year-round in Maine. Between migrants and resident species, approximately 145 known breeding bird species inhabit Maine.

Terrestrial mammals attract less attention than birds simply because most are nocturnal. Like birds, most of Maine's terrestrial mammals are found throughout the state. Fifty-two species of mammals inhabit the coastal region. Of these 52, all are year-round residents except three species of bats that migrate southward for the winter.

Several species such as the New England cottontail, pine vole, gray fox and Virginia opossum reach the northern limits of their ranges along the Maine coast. However, most species—such as moose, black bear, pine marten and others—are widely distributed in northern New England as well as across all of Canada in the boreal forest belt.

Most of these mammals are still relatively common. The black bear, however, has seen increasing human encroachment into its habitat. Once found along the entire Maine coast, today black bears rarely turn up south of Penobscot Bay. They become progressively more common the farther east one travels. Primarily vegetarians, bears relish meat when available. In the early years of European settlement, bears found abundant food resources along the seacoast: fish, carrion from dead whales, seals and other sea mammals and, reportedly, lobsters caught in tide pools!

Two mammals fared even worse than the black bear. Farmers eradicated the wolf because it ate meat—both wild and, especially, domestic. Fear of wolf predation led many settlers to clear offshore islands for wolf-free pastures or domestic livestock. As early as 1640, Maine paid bounties on wolves. The diligent efforts of Maine's inhabitants exterminated wolves from the coast as well as the interior of Maine by the 1800s.

The sea mink, a slightly larger version of the freshwater mink, once roamed Maine's coast. Although early settlers did not hate the sea mink as much as the wolf, it was a valuable fur-bearer—so valuable that trapping led to its extinction sometime around the Civil War. Today, the

niche of the sea mink has been partially filled by the mink, which is found across the country.

ISLAND BIOGEOGRAPHY

Nineteen species of rodents are known to inhabit coastal Maine. They vary in size from the beaver and porcupine down to the meadow vole and deer mouse. Most people never even see the smaller mammals—voles, mice and bog lemmings—yet the natural distribution of these species on Maine's coastal islands led to the development of one of the more important principles of modern conservation biology—the theory of island biogeography.

The theory holds that all populations undergo natural fluctuations in numbers, sometimes going locally ex-

Coastal raised bogs or heaths are unique plant communities with poor drainage dominated by eastern larch, black spruce, blueberry and sphagnum moss. They are found only in a narrow strip within 10 miles of the coast between Acadia National Park and West Quoddy Head State Park.

Lily pads at Ames Pond, Stonington.

tinct. Due to these random extinctions, the smaller the original population, the more likely it is to go extinct. Larger islands can usually provide more habitat, and thus host larger populations of each species that originally colonized the island. Larger islands also tend to contain more potential niches for different species. All things being equal, smaller islands should have fewer species than larger ones.

Ken Crowell developed the concept of biogeography. A zoology student who inventoried rodent populations on Deer Isle and the nearby Merchant Row Islands between Stonington and Isle au Haut, Crowell discovered that the larger Deer Isle was home to three rodent species—the meadow vole, deer mouse and red-backed vole—while only the meadow vole inhabited the smaller islands of

Merchant Row. Crowell introduced the missing species to the smaller Merchant Row Islands, and then reinventoried their population status over time; both the deer mouse and red-backed vole populations became extinct, while the meadow vole continued to thrive.

The reason for the difference lay in each species' survival strategies. In an average year, meadow voles, very prolific breeders, produce 233 offspring in the time red-backed voles can produce only 25. On the mainland, or a larger island, a species with a low breeding potential like the red-backed vole can easily supplement its local populations by recruitment from nearby populations, but on an island the possibilities are more limited.

Crowell found that competition between the deer mouse and meadow vole differed from that between the meadow and red-backed voles. The deer mouse breeds as prolifically as the meadow vole. However, its diet differs. It eats primarily seeds and fruits, and so must forage over larger territories than the stem- and leaf-munching meadow vole must cover. On smaller islands, food availability and the time required to obtain food doomed the deer mouse. As a consequence of these different ecological strategies and niche selection, neither the red-backed vole nor the deer mouse can compete effectively against the meadow vole on small islands.

In recent years, Crowell's basic idea has been refined to describe not only physical islands, but also any habitat that is limited or discontinuous. Thus a moist mountain surrounded by desert functions as an "island" to animal populations just as the real islands of Merchant Row.

The more mobile an animal, the more likely that it will be found on islands. For example, whitetail deer are abundant and quite common, especially on the larger offshore islands like Mount Desert Island. They cross the ice to islands in winter, and have been known to swim 10 miles across open water. Moose also occasionally inhabit offshore islands. However, moose need larger foraging territories than deer and can sustain breeding populations on only the largest islands.

THE WATERY REALM

Just as the land's own environmental parameters influence what can live where, the sea presents unique living problems and solutions. Unlike the land, the sea maintains remarkable environmental stability. Temperature, a major influence on animal and plant distribution on land, remains more constant in the ocean. Temperature changes still influence many marine animals, however. Fluctuations in lobster, mackerel and other populations correlate directly with sea-water temperature changes. The average year-round water temperatures off Maine vary as much as 9° Fahrenheit, according to permanent records begun in 1906. Until 1940, the mean annual water temperatures were below 47°. However, since this date, the waters have warmed slightly and allowed plants and animals that require a warmer environment to move farther north, while cold-adapted species have had to retreat.

Ocean plants and animals must contend not only with long-term temperature trends, but also with relatively dramatic seasonal variations. At Boothbay Harbor, seasonal temperatures vary by nearly 50°, ranging from a low of 28° to a high of 73°. Tides also affect temperatures— the tremendous turbulence created by the giant tides in the Bay of Fundy reduces the difference between high and low temperatures. As any resident of Washington County can attest, waters in the Bay of Fundy tend to be cooler in summer than those of areas farther south, primarily because colder deep waters are regularly brought to the surface by tide mixing.

BETWEEN THE TIDES

Tidal range also influences marine organisms. In the tropics the difference between high and low tides may amount to no more than one or two feet. As a consequence, environmental conditions are nearly homogeneous for animals or plants there. However, in Maine the tidal zone ranks among the largest in the world, and it increases from south to north. For example, Portland's tidal range

Tidal zonation showing the white barnacle and darker rockweed zone. The plants and animals that live in each zone depend in a large part upon their ability to withstand desiccation and pounding surf.

averages nine feet, while Eastport's averages 18.2 feet. Almost nowhere else in the world does an intertidal region offer more diversity than the Maine coast: numerous rocky bowls, coves and shelves in which animals and plants can hide, scuttle or cling. In addition, solid rockbound coast provides firm attachment surfaces for those plants and animals that must withstand the crashing surf.

Animals and plants that live in the intertidal zone, such as seaweeds, snails, mussels and periwinkles, face a variety of environmental stresses not found in the open sea. When the tide is out, organisms must cope with the same stresses encountered on land, including summer heat, freezing winter temperatures and desiccation by winds. Any species colonizing this zone must be able to tolerate all these extremes, plus survive pounding surf and submersion.

Perhaps more than any other factor, ice determines which species survive in the intertidal zone. In regions where winter ice is common, the churning action of frozen chunks can scrape away most intertidal organisms.

Why, then, does any animal or plant occupy such an obviously harsh environment? The answer in nearly all cases is that they thereby avoid most other potential competitors and predators. In addition, tidal areas, awash in surf, offer abundant food and oxygen.

Although all species in this zone have adapted to the stressful intertidal environment, some tolerate prolonged periods of exposure better than others. As a result, zonation is apparent in tidal areas, with species least tolerant of exposure living in the lowest zone while those most tolerant inhabit the upper limits of the intertidal region.

Peer down into a tide pool. An incredible, action-packed, grisly drama is being played out there. Predators stalk prey. Species battle each other for food, space and shelter. But you must be attuned to the action to notice the players.

The highest tidal zone, the black "scum" layer, looks like a kind of dirty bathtub ring on rocks near the high-water line. Only occasionally do tides submerge it. On first glance, you might assume it is only a water stain. However, try walking on it when it's wet. You will (sometimes abruptly) discover it is rather like a coating of ice: very slick. The stain is, in fact, a living band of blue-green algae, some of the most primitive plants in the world. Able to photosynthesize, but lacking nuclear membranes, they resemble bacteria more than anything else. Their slippery surface results from a mucus-like substance that protects them from desiccation when exposed at low tides.

Due to extreme environmental conditions in this zone, few creatures survive here. The blue-green algae has only one predator: a half-inch-long snail, the rough periwinkle, which grazes on the algae when it is wet, rasping the plants off the rock with a rough tongue called a radula.

The rough periwinkle is halfway through its evolution into a land snail. A lung-like organ allows it to live for long periods outside its watery home. However, to avoid desiccation, periwinkles crowd into rock cracks. They can live as long as a month out of water by tightly sealing their shells to the rocks. Surprisingly for a marine organism, a periwinkle actually drowns if submerged too long.

Another adaption to its near-terrestrial existence is live birth. Unlike other species of periwinkles, which lay eggs in the watery zones below, young rough periwinkles develop inside their mothers and are born as miniature versions of their parents.

Contrasting markedly with the black zone is the next level, a broad white band: the barnacle zone. Barnacles look something like mussels and clams with six-sided limestone shells, but they are really arthropods—the same group as insects. Instead of hard internal skeletons, arthropods posses an exoskeleton (or outer skeleton) encasing the body. Marine arthropods are known as crustaceans, include such familiar creatures as lobsters, crabs and shrimp.

The barnacle's six-plated shell helps disperse the energy of crashing surf and allows the barnacle to survive what would otherwise prove an inhospitable environment. Snug inside its tiny shell house, the barnacle sticks out its feet to sweep in food when water covers it. By withdrawing its feet and closing its shell during low tide, it can survive long periods of exposure to drying air, and even freezing temperatures. In addition, a barnacle can breathe air through a small opening in its shell. However, if exposed too long to drying air, the barnacle will close its shell completely and may suffocate.

Young barnacles look nothing like adults. From tiny larva floating randomly through the sea, they gradually grow and periodically shed their exoskeletons. Eventually, each larva selects a substrate—be it the rocky coast, the bottom of a ship or a pier pile—and then secretes a very strong glue to cement itself to the chosen site, where it will remain the rest of its life. Gradually the barnacle grows its shell and settles into a life of eating and mating.

Right: Red squirrels are common in the spruce and pine forests of the coast.
Below: Whitetail deer fawn. Whitetail deer are common all along the coast and even on many offshore islands, which they reach over the ice in winter or even by swimming.

Right: Rock crab, a common resident of tidal pools and rocky coastlines
Below: Low tide at Crescent Beach. Exposed are green Irish moss and various kelp, including bladderwrack and rockweed.

Stalking the barnacle is the predatory dog whelk. At the lower end of the barnacle zone, where submergence is more common, dog whelk—not so well-adapted for life in the open air as the barnacle—can ravage a barnacle colony. The abundance of predatory dog whelk keeps barnacles from invading lower tidal zones. Since dog whelk and other barnacle predators like the starfish are bottom creepers, barnacles find boats attractive and safe, since none of their customary predators threatens them there.

Don't look for an action-packed chase between predator and prey in a tide pool. No wolves chase caribou here. Instead, the dog whelk meticulously chooses its sedentary prey, selecting larger barnacles, then secretes a poison that kills the crustacean. The barnacle's muscles relax after it dies, and then the dog whelk easily pries open the barnacle and feasts on its soft tissues.

Battling barnacles for space on the rocks are mussels, steel-blue bivalves related to clams. However, unlike clams, which burrow in soft mud or sand, mussels attach themselves to rocks or any other solid substrate by secreting a thin, flexible protein material that hardens on contact with salt water. Thin line by thin line, the mussel firmly attaches itself with a web of fine strands.

Like that of the barnacle, the mussel's shape blunts the blows of pounding surf. One end, narrower than the other, slices the oncoming surge like the prow of a ship.

Inhabiting the upper levels of tide zones, mussels survive exposure to air for hours. When the tide retreats, a mussel closes its shell tightly, enhancing the seal with a soft layer of tissue along the shell's edge, much like a rubber gasket.

Mussels often compete with barnacles for desirable locations on rocks. Often, over the course of a summer, mussels gradually replace barnacles in a site that was covered with the white crustaceans during spring. When you find steel-blue mussels intermixed with white barnacles, you have discovered a slow battle for turf; usually by summer's end the mussels win. So why don't mussels eventually replace barnacles completely? The answer lies in predation.

The mussel is a popular dinner item among a host of predators. At the lower end of the intertidal zone, both starfish and crabs consume mussels. Neither ventures too far from the low tidal zone, though, so they mainly frequent the lower edge of a mussel colony. But other predators work the upper limits of a mussel colony. Gulls, oystercatchers, raccoons and many other animals keep mussels from overrunning the upper ends of barnacle zones.

Ice and severe winter cold also can kill whatever barnacles and mussels escape predators, thus cleaning rock surfaces so that, by spring, they can invite renewed colonization by these animals.

Below the white barnacle zone and extending down to the mean low-water mark, great clusters of brown algae we commonly call "seaweed" cover the rockweed zone—slick and slimy at low tide, covered with water at high tide.

Waving gently in the surf when the tide covers them, many rockweed species use tiny buoys to float their leaves close to the surface where light for photosynthesis is greater. Unlike land plants, plants of the sea do not need extensive root systems for gathering nutrients. The water surrounding them provides abundant minerals. Rockweeds have holdfasts instead of roots, which anchor the plants to rocks or other firm surfaces.

Four types of rockweed inhabit the intertidal zone. The two most common are bladder wrack (*Fucus vesiculosus*), which dominates the upper half of this zone, where surf action is greatest; and knotweed (*Ascophylum nodosum*), which competes better in more protected sites, and thus is more common at lower levels.

Bladder wrack is easy to recognize: it is tipped with Y-shaped branches and has small bladders along the mid-

ribs of its branches. Knotweed, a long and stringy plant, grows up to 10 feet in length and sports inflated nodules that look like knots on a rope—hence its name.

Two other less common species associated with this zone are *Fucus spiralis* and *Fucus distichus*. The former grows at the highest levels of the rockweed zone. Since it spends most of its time uncovered by the tide, it has no need for flotation and thus lacks gas bladders. At the lower limits of the rockweed zone, nearly always covered by wa-

Barnacles at low tide. They are really arthropods, in the same family as lobsters, crabs and shrimp. Barnacles are one of the most amazing creatures in the intertidal zone. Inside their tightly closed shells, they can withstand freezing temperatures, prolonged exposure to the air and pounding surf.

The dog whelk is a major predator of the intertidal zone. It drills holes into the shells of barnacles and mussels and is a major control on the expansion of these shellfish.

ter, is *Fucus distichus*. It is recognizable by its long flattened fruiting bodies that contain eggs and sperm.

Just below the rockweed zone, a narrow zone of red and green seaweed—the Irish Moss Zone—appears only during the lowest tides of any month. Species that need a more or less continuous watery environment live here: starfish, crabs and sea urchins. Irish moss dominates this zone. This short red algae, usually less than four inches high, is a major source of carrageenin—used as a thickening agent in products like ice cream and pudding.

The competition for space in the desirable lower zone is intense. Both barnacles and mussels compete with Irish

moss for holdfast sites on rocks, and Irish moss usually loses, particularly to mussels. However, allies aid Irish moss in its battle for survival: the predatory dog whelk, starfish and crabs.

The starfish, perhaps the most methodical of these predators, attacks a mussel with its five tube feet, slowly applying pressure, tightening like a vise. The steady pressure usually causes the mussel to open its shell slightly, a fatal mistake. At this point, the starfish inverts its stomach in its mouth area and slips it inside the mussel. Stomach enzymes begin to digest the still-living mussel, and eventually most of the starfish's stomach winds up inside the mussel shell. When its meal is complete, the starfish withdraws its stomach and hunts for another victim.

The lowest tidal zone, visible only during the lowest tides, is the Larminarian, or kelp, zone, named for various species of brown kelp. Sugar kelp grows up to 10 feet long. Horsetail kelp has a wide base that divides into long, slender, finger-like ribbons. One kelp of deeper waters, hollow-stemmed kelp, sometimes reaches 30 to 40 feet.

Like rockweeds, kelps have strong holdfasts, which they attach to rocky bottoms in clear water. Conditions here resemble those of the open ocean except for the ebb and flow of tides. The long strands of kelp form dense beds, marine "forests" where a variety of animals lives—feeding on the kelp or each other.

Just as herbivorous snails graze on algae in the black zone, grazers frequent these lower tidal kelp zones. If you stare into the lowest tide pools near the edge of the kelp zone, you might see what appears to be a three- to four-inch-diameter pincushion. This pincushion, the green sea urchin, relentlessly grazes on kelp and, where the sea urchin thrives, kelp disappears. Lobsters eat sea urchins, but in most intertidal waters heavy commercial harvest has depleted lobster populations. A chain reaction occurs: when we lose the lobsters, we lose the kelp forests and many other fish and plants that find shelter and food among the wavy kelp fronds.

One of the most voracious grazers of kelp is the sea urchin. It is completely covered with green spines except on its bottom, where it attaches to rocks. Besides gulls and some starfish, not many creatures like to eat sea urchins. However, some people have developed a taste for sea urchin gonads, called "sea eggs." If the sea urchin fishery grows enough to reduce sea urchin populations, kelp beds may recolonize many of their former haunts.

SEABIRDS

The numerous offshore islands that speckle the Maine coast provide breeding grounds for feathered abundance—the seabirds that hunt the tidepools, beaches and open oceans. Some seabirds, like gulls and terns, nest on islands but spend most of the year spread out along the coast and even are quite comfortable on inland bodies of fresh water. Others, birds of the open ocean like puffins, auks, shearwaters and petrels, alight on land only once a year when they gather in large breeding colonies.

When the first Europeans arrived on the Maine coast, they noted with awe the immense congregations of breeding birds. Soon they began annihilating birds. The newcomers collected and sold eggs, and shot adult birds to feed themselves or their hogs, or merely for feathers. By 1850, one species, the great auk, was extinct, and many other species seemed doomed to the same fate. Maine's breeding populations of double-crested cormorants, eiders, puffins, black guillemots and greater black-backed gulls disappeared. By the late 1800s the birds received protected status and a slow recovery began. Some species, like puffins, still are absent from many former haunts, while other species—like herring and greater black-backed

Kelp zone exposed at low tide.

Starfish are denizens of deeper tide pools. A major predator on mussels and other shellfish, starfish can quickly eat their way through a mussel colony.

mies. Synchronization of breeding also occurs in colonies. Colony birds produce young at about the same time, and thus may "swamp" predators—in effect, providing far more food than predators can effectively utilize. Enough young survive to assure the colony's continued existence.

Two other traits characterize seabirds: their typically small clutch size and the participation of both parents in raising young. The dangers of predation require that one parent guard the young almost constantly while, simultaneously, the growing chicks demand large and constant supplies of food. Parents must work together to successfully raise a brood. In addition, the high energy costs of raising a brood preclude big families. A puffin, for example, usually lays one egg, and even gulls and terns produce no more than two or three. With the "investment cost" in each chick so high, it is not surprising that seabirds, unlike many other animals, tend to be monogamous.

In addition, since it requires quite a bit of experience to successfully rear a clutch, most seabirds do not breed until they are three or four years old. Unlike many smaller birds, whose life expectancy rarely exceeds two or three years, seabirds may live 20 to 30 years. As a result of their late sexual maturity and small broods, seabird populations recover slowly from depredation.

It is difficult to believe that the ubiquitous cry of the herring gull once nearly was silenced on the Maine coast. In the 1880s only a few thousand pairs remained, all north of Penobscot Bay. However, with protection their numbers began to increase, slowly at first, then more rapidly. Today they are actually expanding their range southward even to the Carolinas. Successful at scavenging what humans toss away as garbage, in Maine alone they number in the tens of thousands.

Other gull species have also expanded their numbers and ranges. At the turn of the century, the greater black-

gulls—probably exceed their previous numbers. These last two species have learned to exploit human garbage and refuse—a continuously growing food source.

Nesting islands free of both predators and disturbances, yet still near abundant food sources, prompt competition among species for breeding sites. Some seabirds avoid the most intense competition by dividing nesting habitat. For example, puffins and storm petrels burrow in soft soil above cliffs; gulls nest in open, flat areas; the gull-like kittiwakes occupy narrow ledges on the sheerest cliffs.

Biologists speculate why seabirds nest in colonies. Perhaps the instinct to mass together provides mutual defense against predators. Certainly, dozens of eyes rather than than two eyes can better detect the approach of ene-

backed gull, largest seagull in the world, did not venture south of Labrador. Its first sighting in Maine did not occur until 1926. Today, Maine hosts an estimated 6,000 to 7,000 pairs.

However, the success of these gulls has extracted a price from other seabirds. Terns, storm petrels and puffins all have lost ground in their fight for survival as gulls have overrun breeding islands. Terns, in particular, have suffered heavily. Gulls not only eat young terns, but they also often claim the best nesting sites, leaving the terns to poorer habitat. Sometimes the ramifications can be dramatic. In 1977, 1,500 pairs of terns nested on Petit Manan Island and, four years later, largely due to competition from the gulls, none could be found. Ornithologist Bill Drury estimated that during the last 10 years populations of island nesting terns declined 40 to 50 percent.

Another bird apparently losing population due to competition and predation by gulls is the infrequently-seen Leach's storm petrel. Except for a small colony in Massachusetts, Maine represents the southern breeding limit of this bird in the United States. Only a few of the 15 breed-

ing colonies on the Maine coast contain more than a handful of birds. The largest colony, with between 1,000 and 2,000 birds, is found on Matinicus Seal Island.

Leach's storm petrel nests underground, using the same burrow year after year. For a long time, no one knew where they nested because petrels come and go from their burrows only at night.

The petrel lays only one egg. Both parents share incubating responsibilities because food sources often exist far from breeding islands: when a mate leaves the burrow, it usually does not return for two days or more. Not surprisingly, a chick takes a long time to mature.

Reacting to the proliferation of gulls, the U.S. Fish and Wildlife Service began experimental and quite controversial gull-poisoning programs. Many people oppose gull control as inappropriate on national wildlife refuges, while others maintain that humans caused gull high population, and hence humans should intervene.

Four species of terns breed along the Maine coast. All display characteristically pointed wings and tails and the distinctive trait of hovering over water as they search for

A recent immigrant to the Maine coast, the snowy egret gradually has been expanding its northern limits into Maine. Egrets are now a common sight in coastal marshes in southern Maine.

A whale can travel the entire length of the Gulf of Maine in a day or two, so widely spaced sightings may not imply that whales are abundant.

American bittern. A common marsh bird, the bittern lies motionless in the reeds until a small frog or other creature approaches, at which point the bittern darts with his dagger-like bill to capture the victim.

small fish, their favorite food. Three of these species—arctic, common and rosette—breed together on the same islands. The smallest tern, the aptly named least tern, nears its northern range limits on the Maine coast. It was one of the most abundant terns in North America, but its nesting requirements—sandy beaches—brought it into direct competition with seaside development and coastal recreational use. Now a threatened species over much of its range, it is known to nest only on a few isolated sand beaches here.

The common puffin, known as a sea parrot for its large, bright red, orange and blue bill, also nests in under-ground burrows. Living most of their lives far out at sea, puffins return to the coast only to breed, arriving in late March or early April. For six weeks or more after their single egg hatches, the adults are model parents, patiently stuffing the young puffin with fish twice a day. Then, before the youngster's flight feathers even mature, they abandon their progeny forever. The chick lives off its fat reserves for a week or more while its feathers fully develop, then it finds its way out of the burrow, usually at night, falls to the ocean in a flurry of wing beats and somehow, without any instruction, learns to fish, fly, swim and survive on its own.

Seeing the adult puffin fly is an unforgettable and, for most people, amusing experience. Puffins excel under the sea's surface where, like penguins, they use their wings to "fly" through the water. In air flight, their tiny wings barely provide enough lift and the chunky birds must beat their wings furiously to stay airborne. If they stop their anxious wing beat, they do not glide, but plummet from the sky. Their landings are usually awkward crashes punctuated by bouncing tumbles.

Puffins, like so many other seabirds, suffered dramatic population declines due to ruthless exploitation by early Maine settlers. By the 1880s only one breeding colony of puffins remained in Maine. A concerted effort to reintroduce puffins on several offshore islands began in 1973. Since puffins return to islands where they were raised, scientists transplanted baby puffins from Newfoundland to Eastern Egg Island and other locations, then carefully hand-fed the young until they matured and flew away. Finally, after years of transplants, some adults did indeed return. To stimulate breeding, scientists erected small wooden decoys complete with mirrors to look like an established colony of puffins. In 1981, the first successful breeding of puffins in more than a hundred years took place on Eastern Egg Island and the tiny population is slowly increasing.

The golden plover, a shorebird of the far north, is occasionally seen on the Maine coast during migrations.

MARINE MAMMALS

Whales provide a rare and unforgettable treat for the Maine coastal visitor and dweller alike. Spying the spout of a blowing cetacean brings out the latent sea captain in all of us. Once common throughout the world, whales were hunted to near-extinction. Even today, a few nations—Japan, the USSR and Norway—still hunt whales for "scientific research." Not wanting to waste the meat after the animals are killed (after science is served), the whales are processed for dog food, cosmetics and other essentials of human happiness and welfare. Perhaps, in the not-too-distant future, "scientists" in these countries will not require hundreds of dead whales a year for their research.

Although 21 species of whales and porpoises inhabit Maine waters, only three whale species—the humpback, minke and finback—and the harbor porpoise are considered common to the Gulf of Maine, and these only seasonally. Most migrate here for the summer, and like most tourists, head for warmer climes with the coming of winter in mid-November. A whale can travel the entire length of the Gulf of Maine in a day or two, so widely spaced sightings do not necessarily imply that whales are abundant.

The most common whale in Maine is the finback, with an estimated North Atlantic population of between 5,000 and 10,000 individuals. Humpbacks are much rarer and there may be fewer than 1,500 in the entire North Atlantic!

The only other marine mammals likely to be seen on the coast are harbor and gray seals. Most gray seals seen in Maine are transients from Canada. Harbor seals far outnumber them. Until 1972, Maine allowed seal hunting and even offered bounties, presumably because they eat commercial fish. Then, in 1972, the Marine Mammals Protection Act protected seals, whales and the like from human predation. In most places, marine mammals have

43

Although able to live at sea for long periods of time, harbor seals still give birth on land. Females produce one pup in the spring after leaving the company of other seals. The pup, usually born on a secluded rocky ledge in one of Maine's many estuaries, swims within hours of its birth. Pups remain with their mothers for six weeks or less before they are weaned. During this critical period, they must acquire sufficient fat reserves to sustain them through the next half year or so while they learn to capture prey.

Starvation, accidents and a host of other mortal dangers claim more than a quarter of the young seals born each year before their first birthdays. However, if they survive their first year, chances are excellent they will live a normal life span of 20 to 30 years.

Groups of seals congregate at favored "haul-out" ledges, where they rest and sun themselves—not unlike many humans who visit the Maine coast for much the same reason. And like some humans, seals tend to return year after year to the same ledge, sometimes even to the same spot on the ledge, but will abandon a favored haul-out if disturbed too frequently.

Many of Maine's coastal animals have suffered directly from human abuses; other resources, such as kelp beds, have been indirectly affected. Fortunately, much of the ecological damage to the Maine coast inflicted by short-sighted human activity is beginning to heal. However, coastal development continues to erode important habitat, and other problems have not gone away. It is time for a new, gentler co-existence with the earth. Considering the biological richness of the Maine coast and its nearby waters, there is probably no better place in the world to begin.

made remarkable comebacks. Now, once again, fishermen are demanding to kill seals.

Seals catch fish by diving underwater and chasing down their prey. Remarkably agile and quick, a seal can drop its heart-rate from 80 beats per minute to 10 beats when diving. Oxygen flow to the brain continues, but the rest of the animal's muscles incur a large oxygen debt.

Harbor seals hauled out on rocks to sun. Although the adults can survive at sea, young always are born on shore—preferably on isolated rocky islets. Once hunted mercilessly, protection by the Marine Mammals Act has allowed harbor seals to recover their numbers over much of the Maine coast.

MAINE'S FISHERIES

Gold and silver, plus a passage to China, originally attracted European explorers to North American shores, but the real "gold" and "silver" discovered in Maine turned out to be the fish that swam off its coast. In the early 1600s, fishermen from Britain, Spain, Portugal and other European nations began to tap the rich fishing grounds of the Grand, Georges and Cape Sable banks.

Fish flourish in this region. The Gulf of Maine occupies an area where currents and upwelling nutrient-rich waters bathe the shallow offshore shoals fishermen call "banks." These physical features, combined with the scalloped coast and its myriad shallow estuaries, provide perfect habitat for young fish and marine invertebrates. In addition, the stable temperatures of the gulf, compared to the nearby mid-Atlantic, support a greater population of resident fish.

Some fish species migrate northward to Maine with the warming waters of summer. These include spiny dogfish, red hake, white hake, American shad, striped bass, bluefish, Atlantic mackerel and bluefin tuna. Others typify the cold North Atlantic, like the herring and cod.

The first fish of commercial importance on the Maine coast was cod. Fishermen caught cod with hand lines and packed it in salt brine or dried it to be shipped to Europe. Cod remains a very important commercial fish in Maine, ranking fifth in 1987 in total catch value.

People were slow to colonize this promising coast because of Indian attacks and border disputes with European nations as well as Canada. Maine's commercial fisheries remained small until after the American Revolution, when Congress voted to provide a subsidy to the American cod fishing industry to encourage its growth. To qualify, a vessel had to fish four months of the year. The subsidy doubled Maine's fishing fleet between 1797 and 1807. By 1860 Maine's fisheries were the second most valuable in the nation. But just after the Civil War, the government cut its subsidy and, within five years, the number of boats in the Maine cod fishing industry declined by half. By the turn of the century, the offshore cod fishery was nearly gone.

In more recent years, fishing techniques changed and larger boats began dragging huge nets to capture cod, as well as other ground fish such as pollock, haddock, hake and cusk. Another relatively recent technique involves gill nets. Gill nets kill not only fish, but also non-target species such as dolphins, seals and even whales. The nets use a series of monofilament meshes with floats on the top and lead weights below. Fish unknowingly swim into the nets and in attempting to escape often catch their gills on the thin line. There they die from asphyxiation. Unfortunately, many of these nets, lost in storms, continue to kill marine mammals and fish for years.

Herring (canned small herring are sardines), a much smaller fish than cod, dominated the Maine fishing industry in the late 1800s. Because they travel in huge schools, herring can be caught easily in large numbers. They are particularly abundant in the Gulf of Maine, especially in the easternmost parts in and around Passamaquoddy Bay.

Facing page: Old and new boats at Stonington's harbor. Maine's rich fisheries were a New World treasure attracting early European explorers.

Lobster traps at Bass Harbor. Until recently, most fishermen constructed their wooden traps during the winter; however, increasingly, the more durable but costlier steel traps are replacing the old wooden trademark of the lobster industry.

Fishermen catch herring by a number of methods. The earliest required simply holding a torch over water at night, when herring move with the tide to feed in shallow coves and bays. The fish, attracted by the light, were easily scooped up with nets or buckets. A slightly more sophisticated method in-volved building a weir across the mouth of a cove, low enough to allow passage of a herring school at high tide, but high enough to trap fish when the tide went out. Today, most herring are caught by pursers. A purser sur-rounds a school of herring with a large net, gradually closes off or "purses" the bottom of the net, and then pulls the net tighter and tighter until the entire school is trapped in a very small area. At this point, a pump extracts the fish into the ship's hold to either become sardines or lobster bait.

Eastport boasted one of the first herring packing plants, producing smoked sardines as early as 1808. By 1900, 68 sardine facto-ries operated in Eastport alone, and sardines ranked second in the nation among canned fish varie-ties in value and volume, exceeded only by salmon.

The rich Gulf of Maine waters produce tremen-dous quantities of herring. The largest catch, totaling 219 million pounds, oc-curred in 1946. In 1987, herring still led all Maine fish in volume, but ranked 14th in value behind lob-ster, shrimp and cod and other species.

Maine's large commer-cial catch has other conse-quences for the ecological fabric of the state's coast. Herring feed nearly every other predator in the ocean, including puffins, gulls, seals, salmon, whales and cod. Therefore, de-clining numbers of herring send serious repercussions throughout the marine ecosystem.

In 1987 the five most valuable species in terms of price per pound caught in Maine were: lobster, which accounted for more than 40 percent of the total dollars spent on any species, followed by shrimp, soft clams, gray sole and cod.

In terms of direct economic contribution, fishing accounts for only 2.8 percent of Maine's total 1980 personal income. Yet, because fishing tends to be labor-intensive and fishermen purchase many supplies locally (gasoline, boats, nets and other gear), the economies of many small coastal communities depend on fishing.

But the importance of fishing goes beyond mere economics. The Maine coast without fishing villages and without fishermen would be a poorer place, socially as well as economically. The fishing industry provides a means of self-employment that requires skill and hard work, but not necessarily a college degree. When, and if, fishing becomes so expensive that fishermen can no longer operate their own small businesses and must become employees, then much will be lost, even if the fishing industry itself remains viable.

Right: Metal lobster pots can be seen on the wharf at Stonington.
Top: Buoys at Cutler.

History

CHAPTER 4

Humans have periodically inhabited Maine at least since the Ice Age glaciers retreated some 10,000 years ago. The earliest residents were big-game hunters, tracking and killing Ice Age mega-fauna like the wooly mammoth.

The world's oceans began to rise again 5,000 years ago, following the Ice Age, and gradually inundated coastal aboriginal sites. Many sites older than 5,000 years are gone, leaving us with an incomplete picture of human use of the coastal environment. Nevertheless, archaeologists have uncovered some surprising information in the artifacts and areas available to them. For example, whitetail deer kills outnumbered moose kills 50 to one in 4,000-year-old sites. Over a long span of time, moose kills became more common: 1,000-year-old sites contain the remains of 21 moose per 100 deer. Scientists attribute this change to a new climate and, hence, new vegetation. Deer favor milder climates and hardwoods, while cooler climates and spruce-fir forests are likely to be dominated by moose.

The warming climate of some 4,000 to 5,000 years ago also is indicated by the fish species commonly found among archaeological remains. For example, at one time Indians caught swordfish, a warm-water species, on the Maine coast. The native people had to continuously adapt to changing climate and available food. The bow and arrow, a fairly recent invention, seems to have been adopted by coastal Indians only a thousand years ago at most. Farming, an even more recent cultural innovation in New England, appeared among Maine coastal tribes at about the time of the first European contact.

Above: Catching, cleaning, salting and drying codfish, from a Herman Moll map of the early 1700s.
Facing page: Sunrise over Frenchman Bay viewed from Mount Desert Island.

Fishermen in dories haul a net in a weir, or fish trap, circa the 1890s, possibly in the area of Lincolnville.

The aboriginal people who greeted the first Europeans were a branch of the Algonquins known as Abnaki. Whether they were direct descendants of the original Ice Age hunters or recent immigrants, we do not know. However, we do know the Abnaki lived in small family groups scattered all along the coast. They relied on coastal resources such as clams, oysters, lobsters, seal and fish, but also hunted deer, moose and other land animals. Although they lived along the coast, they never developed a maritime tradition as did Indians of the Northwest, where whales and other marine resources were more important to the cultures.

European contact with these Maine Indians occurred very early. Thirty-two years after Columbus bumped into the Caribbean in his epic 1492 journey, Giovanni da Verrazano, sailing for the French, traded with Indians along the southern coast of Maine. (Things did not go especially well for him, so he called the area "The Land of the Bad People.") Other explorers followed, seeking riches. It soon became apparent that the Maine coast did not offer a passage to China or gold and silver, but held other riches.

By the early 1600s, fishermen from Normandy, Britain, Portugal and Spain were sailing across the Atlantic to exploit North America's Grand Banks and other rich fisheries. These fishermen frequently dried fish on offshore islands before sailing back to Europe. Although battles between whites and Indians would divide the two races later in history, there is no record of hostilities between these fishermen and the Indians. But formal hostilities matter little, for the Europeans brought a scourge worse than warfare: disease.

The first recorded epidemic raced through many New England tribes between 1616 and 1618, and devastated Maine's Indian people in 1617-1618. Smallpox epidemics continued to wrack Maine's Abnaki; other outbreaks were recorded in 1639 and 1646. As a result, when the first whites attempted to settle on Maine's coast they encountered little resistance from the native people. There were few left to put up a determined fight.

A small island with red rock shorelines, near Calais in the middle of the St. Croix River, now lies at the border of Maine and New Brunswick, Canada. Across the water, it seems quiet and undistinguished from thousands of other islands dotting the Maine coastline. However, it was St. Croix Island that the Frenchman Pierre de Guast, Sieur de Monts, selected in June 1604 by as the location for the first government-sponsored colonial venture, one of France's first New

France chose St. Croix Island in 1604 for one of its first New World settlements.

A peaceful, calm morning at Castine belies its turbulent past. The village underwent nine changes in national ownership, with French, English, Dutch and Americans all vying for possession of this important port.

Fort Knox, at Bucksport, protected the upper end of the Penobscot Bay.

colony collapsed after one winter—not because of the weather, but primarily because the colony's chief sponsor died and funding ended.

The French made another attempt at colonization in what would become Maine, settling on Mount Desert Island (today's Acadia National Park) near Fernald Point at the entrance to Somes Sound. An Englishman, Captain Samuel Argall, who had orders to evict all foreigners from English colonial soil, attacked the settlement known as St. Sauveur. The French fled.

In 1622, Edward Winslow of the Plymouth, Massachusetts colony, stopped at Damariscove Island, and reported more than 30 ships there. The year-round fishing station established just that year was solely a work site for employees of English investors. Men who were single came to work, with no intention of making Maine their home. The station's supplies arrived from England, and it returned cured fish. Similar stations arose at nearby Cape Newagon and at Piscataqua and, briefly, at Monhegan beginning the following year, and at Pemaquid in 1625.

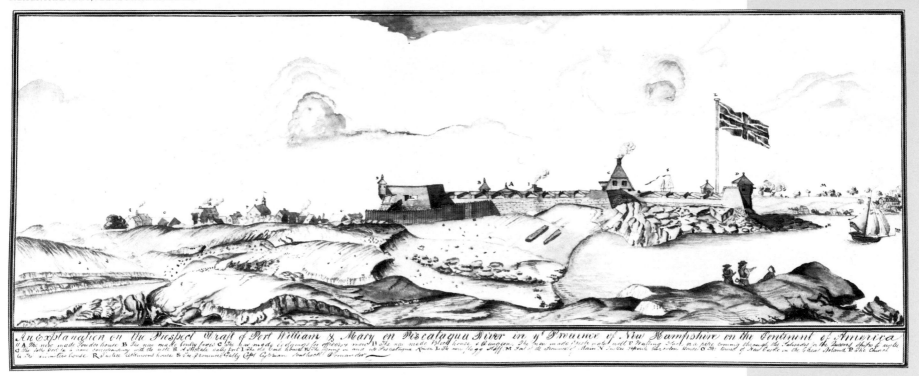

An Explanation on the Prospect Draft of Port William & Mary on Piscataqua River in ye Province of New Hampshire on the Continent of America

True communities of permanent settlers began in the late 1620s with Pemaquid and Damariscove; 1630 saw the foundings of York, Saco and probably Cape Porpoise; Kittery was founded the following year; Scarborough and Casco[Falmouth] began in 1633, North Yarmouth in 1636, and Wells in 1640. These were communities of families, rather than the fishing stations' bachelors, and they farmed for market as well as their own subsistence, trading dairy products, grain and other crops with local merchants. By mid-century, coastal farms were successful enough to export livestock.

But most of Maine's coast remained uninhabited, due to uncertainty about which European power controlled North America: both France and England claimed Maine. Other countries also attempted to settle Maine's shores—between 1626 and the conclusion of the War of 1812, Castine on Penobscot Bay underwent nine changes in national ownership, with French, English, American and Dutch flags flying over this strategic port at various times.

Indian attacks constantly threatened, especially during the French and Indian Wars, which began in 1675 and continued until 1755. The French were only minimally involved in the first of these wars, known as King Phillip's War (1675-1678), but after that incited Indians to attack English settlements. The Indians, alarmed at English encroachment on their territory, thoroughly complied, frequently attacking Maine's fledgling villages.

Maine was part of the northern frontier of the Massachusetts colony and remained so until 1820 when it was granted statehood. Massachusetts used the Maine villages as a buffer, protecting its flanks by encouraging new settlement along the northern borders. Virtually all Maine settlements came under attack and the continual threat to life and property posed by Indians, as well as the changing whims of European political powers, hindered the settlement of Maine for decades.

The first Indian War in 1675 eliminated nearly every farmhouse along the entire southern coast of Maine from Casco Bay to Penobscot Bay. Subsequent wars continued to take their tolls and, by 1713, Maine's white and Indian populations both had declined. In 1720, only one house still stood in the great sweep of coastline from Georgetown

The Union Jack would have been huge at Fort William and Mary if this sketch were to scale. The legend reads: "An Explanation on the Prospect Draft of Port (sic) William & Mary on Piscataqua River in ye Province of New Hampshire on the Continent of America" and identifies the structures. The Maine–New Hampshire border was established to the south, along the Piscataqua River, in a British land grant in 1629.

Above: Constructing the four-masted schooner *Charles D. Stanford* in 1918 at the Bangor-Brewer Shipbuilding Company in Brewer. The man at left is dubbing with an adze: making a flat spot to lay the keels on the floor timbers.
Facing page: Looking across the St. Croix River to St. Croix Island, site of the attempted French settlement in 1604.

to the St. Croix River. The Indian wars ended in the mid-1750s and, by then, the native population had moved far north and inland.

Once the British eliminated the French threat by conquering Quebec in 1759 and Montreal in 1760, concluding the French and Indian Wars, colonists began to move northward onto the Maine coast in greater numbers. Communities like Pemaquid and Sheepscot, abandoned during the years of war, were resettled.

However, the peaceful future these settlers envisioned dissipated as the alliance between the American colonists and the British deteriorated. The King's Broad Arrow edict, for example, reserved all pines larger than 22 inches in diameter for the Royal Navy. (Such trees were marked by chopping an inverted "V" into the bark to make the "arrow" marking.) In its heyday by the mid-1700s the Royal Navy needed tremendous amounts of wood for boat construction. At the same time, England needed wood for

home construction and firewood. The English crown turned from its own overharvested forests to its North American colonies for the wood needed to maintain a naval power.

Royal foresters cruised through the American woods marking all large pine trees as His Majesty's property and infuriating colonists, particularly those on the coast of Maine where some of the most accessible white pine forests in North America existed. Local loggers and sawmill owners in the fledgling timber industry considered all Maine trees their own by proprietary right and they resented the British regulations. Most colonists ignored the law and a surprising number of boards in colonial homes measured just less than 22 inches—sawed from trees with larger girths. The resentment created by the King's Broad Arrow edict was among the many factors that led to the American Revolution.

Most of the Revolution's major battles took place south of Maine, but a few incidents occurred here. For example, Machias was the scene of the first naval battle of the Revolution, and the British Navy bombarded and burned Portland, then called Yarmouth. Fort George at Castine, held by the British, was attacked in 1779 by American forces with a subsequent loss of 44 American vessels and more than 500 lives.

With the end of the revolution, the Maine coast settled into a period of relative prosperity. Shortly after the British surrendered, settlers streamed northward and established most of the villages and towns we know today during the short time between the revolution and the War of 1812.

During the War of 1812, several Maine communities came under British fire and control, including Castine, which changed hands once more. But Maine suffered far worse from the 1807 Embargo Act, which forbade trade with Britain or Canada, than from cannon fire. Maine, economically dependent upon maritime activities, was severely hurt, and opposition to the war was widespread. Smuggling goods into Canada flourished. Although Maine's sympathies initially be-

A lobsterman salting bait at Small Point, 1888.

longed to Britain and Canada, attitudes changed after the British occupied all of Maine from Penobscot Bay to Passamaquoddy Bay in 1814, and Mainers urged the U.S. government to provide protection.

The war ended shortly after this British occupation and Maine quickly rebuilt its maritime commerce. Postwar affluence spawned a movement to separate Maine from Massachusetts. In 1819, voters passed a referendum calling for separation and creation of a new state. However, the issue of slavery hampered approval by the U.S. Congress. At the same time Maine asked for statehood, Missouri also sought admission to the Union. Northern states, anxious to prevent the spread of slavery, stalled Missouri's request while southerners worked to keep Maine out of the Union. Both factions strove to prevent an imbalance in power between northern and southern states. Eventually, Congress hammered out the Missouri Compromise, admitting Missouri as a slave state and Maine as a free state and maintaining balance in the Senate between North and South.

The new state had to clear up another old problem. Its northern boundary with New Brunswick, Canada never had been clearly identified. Nothing was done until 1839, when 205 Canadians "invaded" Maine to cut timber,

prompting some Maine residents to call for war. As Maine prepared for war, negotiations between the Canadian and U.S. governments ended the dispute. In 1842, the Webster-Ashburton Treaty settled the boundary question and Maine acquired its present borderlines.

Despite these setbacks, Maine's population and economy grew rapidly during the early 1800s. The state enjoyed relative prosperity as the rich fishing grounds of the Grand Banks and Georges Banks were fully tapped, and lumbering, farming and ship building developed. Nearly all these products were shipped out of state, hence Maine's economy was based largely on maritime trade and export. Its population grew to 298,000 people by the time of statehood arrived in 1820.

Farming, significant to Maine's economy since earliest settlement despite legends to the contrary, now began to boom. By 1820, there were 31,000 farms in Maine, with 301,000 acres of meadow and 79,000 acres of cultivation. And by 1880, nearly 1.4 million acres along the coast were in agricultural production and there were an estimated 64,000 farms. Much of this farm acreage was devoted to hay production for export. With local transportation relying on horses, cities such as Boston had a tremendous need for hay, and

Maine's coastal farms were a ready source since boat passage took less than 24 hours.

Farm production has declined since the late 1800s and by 1970 there were fewer than 8,000 farms still in cultivation. However, one still finds apple trees growing in many out-of-the-way places that once were farm clearings.

Never far behind farming and fishing as a staple of the Maine coastal economy, lumbering soon rose to provide the state's number-one export. By 1833 the Bangor *Republican* boasted that three fourths of all the white pine in the United States came from Maine. The many large rivers of the state provided both the waterpower necessary for the operation of saw mills and water highways to get timber from the hinterlands to the mills via log drives. Towns like Bangor rapidly became major lumber cities.

While lumbering sought out waterfalls for mill sites, the potential power of these rivers also was tapped by other industries. Beginning in the 1810s, textile and woolen mills rose on many coastal rivers, with major mills established at Brunswick, Saco and Biddeford in mid-century.

Textile and woolen mills were joined by pulp mills in the 1850s after the invention of the pulp-paper process. This occurred just about when Maine's initial boom in white-pine lumber was ending. The new technology in the paper industry sparked interest in harvesting Maine's heretofore unusable spruce and fir for pulp production. Even more mills sprouted on Maine rivers and coastal commerce benefited from the exports.

During this industrial expansion and with the export of natural resources and finished products, Maine's maritime shipping business enjoyed healthy years. Many of the larger Victorian homes found today in such towns as Kennebunk, Searsport and Castine were built by wealthy ship owners and sea captains who prospered during the heyday of the shipping and sailing era.

Between the Civil War and well into the next century, Maine settled into a period of stagnation and even population decline in many rural areas. Most villagers tended to be somewhat self-sufficient, often blending work on coastal farms with fishing or ship building. The large families they spawned soon filled up the suitable farmland

Abundant waterpower close to coastal harbors led to the development of textile mills on many southern Maine rivers. This old mill is on the Saco River at Biddeford.

Scenic landscapes, such as here on Monhegan Island, contributed to the first tourist rush to Maine in the mid-1800s. Artists and tourists still flock here.

and many sons and daughters had to leave Maine and move westward. Many coastal villages maintained themselves, but did not grow substantially.

The quiet charm of these isolated villages, seemingly stuck in time, appealed to an ever-widening circle of sportsmen, campers, nature lovers and others with the time and money to vacation on the Maine coast. As others did inland, they would board with local farmers and fishermen while soaking in the local color and the beauty of the coast. These "rusticators," as they were called, returned year after year to renew friendships with coastal people and to enjoy the simple life.

Then the development of more rapid transportation, primarily trains and steamboats, put these coastal villages within reach of wealthy city dwellers from Boston, New York and other eastern cities, and bucolic coastal fishing villages became attractive destinations for harried urbanites. At first, the new tourists followed the example of the earlier rusticators and boarded with local fishermen and their families, but as their numbers increased, new, often more elegant, facilities were built to meet their needs. Large inns sprouted in the more popular destinations to cater to summer "guests" who spent their days admiring the sea from the comfort of wicker chairs and rockers on wide porches. For the more active there were badminton, tennis, yacht-

ing and beachcombing. Mount Desert Island's Bar Harbor, an early popular resort community, had 17 hotels by 1887.

Some of these people began to buy coastal property and build summer "cottages." These extravagant structures were often very large, and frequently had formal flower gardens, with clipped, spacious lawns where card games and badminton were played. These summer homes would more properly be called estates. More modest cabins were referred to as "camps," but even these would be considered quite elegant by contemporary standards. Each year, these "summer people" would return to their seaside homes in such communities as Boothbay, Bar Harbor and Northeast Harbor to mix with other socially prominent families like the Rockefellers, Fords, Vanderbilts, Carnegies and Astors. A supplemental economy generated by the demands of wealthy urbanites helped many local inhabitants earn extra income working part-time as innkeepers, boat builders, winter caretakers and boat keepers.

After World War II, the pace of life changed rapidly. The middle class found the Maine coast affordable and accessible due to the rise in affluence, combined with better highways and wide-spread automobile ownership. These people also built summer cottages, but on a decidedly smaller scale than the wealthy vacationers of the previous era. And, rather than spending entire summers on the Maine coast, they often had only two- or three-week vacations.

Adding to the summer residents were the highly mobile tourists, coming to Maine for a weekend or a few weeks at most, filling the numerous hotels and motels that began to line the coastal arteries. All these newcomers sought the same qualities of Maine's coast that first attracted the rusticators. Driving the blacktopped two lanes to the small villages, they too revelled in the timelessness of the lighthouses, the lobster traps and buoys piled on wharves and the fishing boats anchored in out-of-the-way harbors. Yet much of what passes as

Village green at Castine. Old, graceful New England homes dominate Castine, which has had a long tradition of maritime wealth.

quaintness, such as the unpainted lobster house and the small quiet stable community, is just another face of poverty. Young people have few employment opportunities and must leave their home towns behind, while those who stay are stuck in unstimulating jobs.

Tourism has become a driving force in many local economies, creating more jobs and perhaps a future for some where there was none before. Nonetheless, tourism has its costs. Traffic jams clog many coastal towns, and shoreline property values have risen so high that many Mainers find themselves priced out of their own communities. Towns are overrun in summer, then boarded up in winter, becoming virtual ghost towns much of the year. At least the relative poverty provided a kind of stability that does not exist in the modern tourist-oriented community.

However, there may be a third choice. Besides offering a poor but unchanging economic backwater, or a fast-paced, transient "community" based on serving outsiders, Mainers can increasingly choose to welcome people who stay. Those who come to Maine to live are retirees; they are also innovative entrepreneurs interested in setting up small, sustainable businesses. In many ways they bring a kind of stability and economic opportunity not found in either of the former choices. Whether Maine can lift itself above the tackiness and flimsiness of the types of development that have overtaken other coastal regions farther south, and continue to provide affordable housing and liveable communities, remains to be seen. However the changes come, the Maine coast, which has sustained and nurtured human beings for nearly 10,000 years, likely will continue to be an attractive and rich environment for generations to come.

Southwest

*T*he Southwest coast subregion begins at Kittery on the New Hampshire border and includes Casco Bay and Portland (pop. 65,000), Maine's largest city. Here the "rockbound" Maine coast recalls those sand-strewn tidelands farther south, in New Jersey, say, or North Carolina. Of the 78 miles of sand beach on the Maine coast, most are strung along the Southwest region: Ogunquit, Moody, York Beach, Old Orchard Beach and others. Unlike the coast farther north, here the shoreline is relatively straight, with few islands and only an occasional rocky headland like Cape Neddick or Cape Porpoise. Only in Casco Bay itself does the popular image of Maine's rugged, island-studded coast match reality.

The vegetation here also differs from the standard for the Maine coast—the spruce-fir forest that dominates coastal areas north of Penobscot Bay. This type of forest barely exists south of Cape Elizabeth. Instead, the Southwest nourishes species usually found in the warmer climate of southern New England. Some of Maine's largest stands of red and white oak grow here, for example. White pine dominates, except in sandy places where pitch pine is more common. In all, some 26 species of plants that typify more southerly locales occur in York County. (These include several found at sites some distance inland.)

The relatively milder climate of the Southwest coast, its sandy beaches and proximity to southern New England, have made this region number-one in tourism and economic growth in the state. Interstate 95 provides particularly rapid and convenient access to the "vacationland" of thousands of weary urbanites. The Southwest coast records the highest per-capita income and employment in the state, and still is growing, sustained by expansion in the electronics, plastics and service industries. Jobs in the service industry now comprise 75 percent of total employment, not all of them low-paying retail positions: for example, the service sector includes professionals in the practice of law, computer consulting, education and communications.

While service businesses saw considerable growth, employment in Maine's more traditional industries, such as textile, leather and paper manufacturing, along with logging, declined. New industries, attracted by Maine's quality of life, have more than compensated for these losses, particularly in the Southwest coast region. For example, by 1986 the unemployment rate for the York-Kittery area hit 1.4 percent, and in the Portland metropolitan area, only 2.6 percent. These rates fall far short of both the national and statewide averages.

As employment opportunities rise, so does demand for housing, shopping malls and other developments. If a land rush is on in Maine, then the Southwest Coast is at the heart of it. In 1960, the population of York County, the fastest growing in the state, totaled 90,402 but by 1986 it had risen to 155,200. Between 1970 and 1980 the county added more than 18,200 new housing units. The Town of York saw some $20 million in land sold to developers in the second half of 1985 and real estate sales have skyrocketed by 400 percent since then! Here, in the most developed portion of the state, towns like York, Kennebunkport and Wells, inundated by rapid subdivision and land development, have enacted building moratoriums to give themselves time to develop land-use plans.

Facing page: Fishing boats at Kennebunkport. Once the home of 30 shipyards, Kennebunkport has become a favorite among "summer people" including President George Bush, who owns a home here.

Wells National Estuary. One of 15 such reserves in the nation, it protects 1,200 acres of tidal salt marsh near the town of Wells.

The modern land rush has rekindled growth in a region that declined after peaking in the late 1800s. The Southwest coast attracted some of Maine's earliest permanent settlements, and entered the maritime trades early. Kittery, for example, located just across the Piscataqua River from Portsmouth, New Hampshire, arose as a strategic location for shipbuilding. As early as 1650, the availability of large white pine for ship masts prompted the British to select the Kittery area for ship building. And when, in 1798, Congress created a Navy Department, it established the Portsmouth Naval Shipyard here. The industry has continued to play a major role in regional economic activity.

Northeast from Kittery on Route 1A—the main coastal artery—are the Yorks: York Harbor, York Village, York Beach and Cape Neddick. They feature many 18th-century historic buildings, including the Old Gaol Museum—built in 1720 and the oldest public building still in use in English North America. But the village of York predates even the Gaol Museum. Settled in 1630 and awarded a royal charter in 1641, it became the first chartered city in America.

Beyond York stretch the beautiful, long, sandy beaches at Ogunquit, now-private Moody Beach and Wells. All these communities depend on the tourist trade and a growing retirement population. Ogunquit, in particular, has a long history as an art colony and resort. Typical of such communities' seasonal population fluctuations, Wells records a year-round home occupation rate of only 60 percent. Yet, a growing number of people choose to stay in the area year 'round, and Wells saw its population jump 75 percent between 1970 and 1980!

The Wells and Ogunquit beaches, created by longshore currents, provide some of the best examples of barrier spits in the entire state. The dunes beyond the sandy ocean front are critical to beach maintenance; most have been fenced to protect their fragile vegetation from trampling.

Left: Willows Bed and Breakfast is typical of the many small inns that dot the Maine coast, catering to the throngs of visitors who arrive each summer to enjoy the Southwest Coast's beaches.
Below: Wild roses along the Webhannet River at Wells National Estuary, part of the Rachel Carson National Wildlife Refuge.

Barriers spits partially break the force of incoming waves, allowing salt marshes to survive in the backwaters. The daily inundation of nutrient-rich tidal waters in coastal estuaries make salt marshes among the most productive ecosystems in the world. Some of these marshes form part of the Rachel Carson National Wildlife Refuge, established in 1966. Rachel Carson wrote the book *Silent Spring,* published in 1962, which first alerted the public to the dangers of pesticide poisoning and, particularly, its impacts on bird life. Fittingly, this refuge designed to protect birds was named in her honor. When all land purchases are completed, the refuge will encompass nearly 5,000 acres in nine locations along the Southwest coast.

Twelve hundred acres of the Carson Refuge also belong to the Wells Natural Estuarine Research Reserve. The marine reserve, one of only 15 in the country, provides a vital nursery for many saltwater species, including striped bass and flounder. Migratory waterfowl, shorebirds and wading birds all find essential habitat protected here—habitat rapidly being lost to dredging, filling and other encroachments elsewhere on the coast. Of all commercially important Atlantic fish species, an estimated two thirds depend upon estuaries like the Wells Reserve sometime during their life cycles.

Just up the coast from Wells are the communities of Kennebunk and Kennebunkport. Kennebunk Historic District preserves fine Victorian, Colonial, Federal and Greek Revival homes, which harken back to the days of the town's prominence as home port for many prosperous ship captains and builders.

Kennebunkport, once the home of 30 ship yards, has traded its maritime economy for one based on tourism. Long a favorite among "summer people," Kennebunkport gained recent additional fame since President George Bush owns a home here.

On Saco Bay between the Saco and Scarborough rivers lies Maine's longest beach complex. It includes Ocean Park, Old Orchard Beach and Ferry Beach. Condos and cottages line the beach-front property where thousands of beach-lovers throng to prance in the ocean and soak up rays.

Just east of this center of human activity lies the outlet of the Scarborough River, whose waters drain the 3,100-acre Scarborough Marsh, Maine's largest tidal wetlands. In colonial days settlers grazed their cattle on this

Most of Scarborough Marsh, Maine's largest salt marsh, is a special wildlife management area. Some 70 percent of all commercially valuable shellfish and fish are produced in tidal wetlands, yet more than 60 percent of coastal marshes on the Eastern Seaboard have been filled or drained.

salt hay and harvested it for winter forage. But as real estate prices escalated in recent times, pressure to drain such marshlands increased. Indeed, on the eastern seaboard, more than 60 percent of the original tidal wetlands already have met this fate. Yet, biologically speaking, few places produce as much as a salt-marsh complex. Some 70 percent of all commercially valuable shellfish and fish depend on in tidal wetlands and, predictably, destruction of such wetlands has a tremendous impact on our nation's fisheries. In addition, wetlands like Scarborough Marsh provide essential waterfowl habitat. Concern over loss of waterfowl nesting areas prompted the Maine Department of Inland Fish and Wildlife to set aside Scarborough Marsh as a special wildlife management area designed to preserve and protect this important tidal estuary.

Beyond Scarborough Marsh and Cape Elizabeth are Casco Bay and Portland. Settled in 1633, and originally named Falmouth, Portland saw early commercial growth largely in the exports of fish and timber. In 1786, shortly after the revolution, part of Falmouth split off and renamed

itself Portland. The new community quickly became the sixth-largest port in the country.

Portland's growth continued, particularly after Maine separated from Massachusetts in 1820. Portland temporarily served as the state's capital. Today, the city forms the heart of the Greater Portland area, home to nearly 250,000 people and an area of revitalization and growth. For example, local entrepreneurs renovated the Old Port District, once a run-down port facility dominated by empty wharfs and warehouses, and it now features restaurants and specialty shops. Cobblestone streets, old iron lampposts, and brick sidewalks all contribute to the 19th-century feel of the port district.

Nothing adds more to Portland's attractiveness as an ocean-side community than the numerous islands in nearby Casco Bay. Stretching 20 miles from Cape Small to Cape Elizabeth, the bay is dotted with long, thin islands. Their linear orientation, northeast to southwest, shows more-resistant rock forming the tops of ridges after erosion eliminated rock from intervening valleys. Subsequently, rising sea levels flooded all but the highest ridgelines and left today's islands.

Originally the islands of Casco Bay were known as the "Calendar Isles," supposedly because there was one island for every day of the year. However, the name lost popularity when someone discovered that there were only 220 islands! Today Mainers use the name "Casco Bay Islands" to describe the chain. The largest islands include Peaks, Little Diamond, Great Diamond, Chebeague, Cliff, Long and Cushings.

The islands eventually became both seasonal and year-round residences for people working in Portland. Peaks Island registers 1,500 year-round residents, but because the island is only a 17-minute ferry ride away from Portland, its population rises to 6,000 in summer. Chebeague Island, the largest Casco Bay island, has a year-round population of only 400 residents. As with most Maine islands, even those with sched-

uled ferry or boat service, visitor facilities including bathrooms are almost non-existent here.

If you find yourself heading north to camp somewhere in the Maine hinterlands and suddenly burn with desire to buy a new camp stove, tent, pocket knife or map, you can always drive just up the freeway from Portland to L.L. Bean Sporting Goods in Freeport. Open 365 days a year, 24 hours a day, Bean's allows you to browse even on New Year's Eve. Linwood Linwood Bean founded the company in 1912 when he first offered his famous hunting shoe—a rubber-bottom, leather-top creation—by mail order catalog. Today, L.L. Bean is Freeport's largest employer and centerpiece of the town's thriving outlet-store business.

The Southwest Coast is a geological transition zone. North of here the coast becomes more rockbound, while to the south the sandy beaches typical of most of the Eastern Seaboard dominate. The economy and human element here also signal transition. Southwest Maine resembles Massachusetts' modern urbanization and growth much more than the Downeast coast of small fishing villages. Yet the region retains charm in abundance. If you seek the "real" Maine (as people told me countless times), you must continue farther north and east. But the Southwest coast offers a fine introduction.

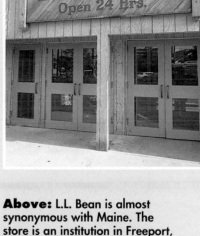

Above: L.L. Bean is almost synonymous with Maine. The store is an institution in Freeport, and open 24 hours a day, seven days a week. It draws shoppers from as far away as Boston.
Left: Downtown Portland. The town has refurbished its historic structures, revitalizing the downtown area.

TIDES

The rhythmic rise and fall of the tide accounts for much of the allure of the ocean. Several factors control tides. Of primary importance, the gravitational pull of the moon, acting with or against the lesser influence exerted by the sun, interacts with the rotation of the earth.

As the earth turns on its axis, the ocean on the side of the planet facing the moon is pulled by the moon's gravitational force. The ocean bulges somewhat, forming a high tide. On the opposite side of the earth, a complementary high tide results from centrifugal force rather than the moon's gravitational pull. Between these two bulges are the low tides.

When the moon and sun align, compounding the gravitational pulls from both sources, they create the highest tides of the month, called "spring" tides. When the moon and sun are at right angles to each other, each somewhat negates the other's effects, and low "neap" tides occur.

Anyone who has watched tides for several consecutive days knows that high and low tides occur 50 minutes earlier each day. This results from the changing position of the moon as it orbits the earth.

As a tide pours into a bay or inlet, it squeezes into progressively narrower passages, creating tidal currents. In some places, these tidal rivers even form rapids or falls as the flood of water drains in or out.

Topography also influences tidal size. The giant 50-foot tides of the Bay of Fundy funnel into progressively narrower channels of the upper bay, forcing the water upward to great height. The 25-foot tides found in Passamaquoddy Bay on the Maine-Canada border also the result from narrowing topography as the tides surge inland.

Right: Surging surf at Mile Beach in Reid State Park. **Facing page:** Low tide at Seawall Beach.

Mid-coast

CHAPTER 6

Many connoisseurs of the Maine coast consider the sandy beaches and summer resort atmosphere of the Southwest Coast illegitimate children of the southlands. To them the "real" coast begins beyond Cape Elizabeth and reaches its most eloquent expression in what is known as the Mid-coast. Here sandy beaches give way to a coast predominantly rock-bound and highly dissected. The Mid-coast area runs from Brunswick to Bucksport on Penobscot Bay and includes numerous long, narrow, rocky peninsulas often separated by narrow cuts and channels.

This is the classic "drowned coast" of Maine, where thin fingers of the sea probe far inland—appearing superficially like the fiord-studded coast of Norway. But the Mid-coast has no real fiords, which are created when glaciers deepen existing river valleys that later are inundated by salt water. To be sure, this portion of Maine endured its share of glaciers, but instead of deepening only valleys, the glaciers overrode everything, leaving behind ample evidence of their passage, including glacial erratics, striations and smoothed and polished bedrock. The sea, due to a world-wide rise in oceans, advanced inland to flood existing river valleys, but the peninsulas and islands that exist today are merely the highest ridges between now-flooded channels and former mouths of the Sheepscot, Kennebec, Damariscotta and St. George rivers.

Because the ocean flooded so many former river valleys, this section contains the greatest percentage of riverine and estuarine wetlands in the state. The largest of these wetlands front the Kennebec, Androscoggin and Sheepscot rivers. Merrymeeting Bay, in particular, formed by the confluence of the Androscoggin, Eastern, Cathance, Muddy, Kennebec and Abagadasset rivers, is the largest freshwater tidal bay north of Chesapeake on the eastern seaboard. Its size alone makes Merrymeeting Bay critical waterfowl habitat and, the establishment of wild rice, an important introduced waterfowl food, has increased the bay's value.

Compared to the Southwest coast, this region has seen less development. Mosaics of pasture and farmland intermixed with forest characterize the Mid-coast. Beech, birch, maple and white pine dominate the woodlands. Except for birch, many of these typical southern New England species give way to northern species farther east beyond Penobscot Bay.

A similar drop-out phenomenon occurs among some marine invertebrates such as American oysters and quahog clams. Dependent upon relatively warm water for growth, they reach their northern limits in the Mid-coast region.

Because its rugged, dissected coast provided abundant natural harbors, this portion of the coast attracted one of the first settlement attempts in Maine, the colony sponsored by Sir John Popham, established in 1607 near the mouth of the Kennebec River and abandoned less than a year later. In 1614, a permanent settlement gained a foothold on the Maine coast; it too was in the Mid-coast region. Beginning as a seasonal fishing station, Damariscove Island soon developed a permanent population that flourished throughout the 1600s. Like many other early coastal ventures, Damariscove exploited the numerous cod fisheries on the Georges Banks.

The earliest fishermen took cod on hook and line; cod were easy to catch and abundant. The lack of oils in their flesh suited them for drying and transport—an important criterion, since Maine shipped most fish to Europe.

Although fishing originally drew European entrepre-

Sunset at Popham Beach.

neurs, the area's coastal rivers soon invited water-powered development. Falls on the Androscoggin River at Brunswick, for example, provided the power for Maine's first cotton mill (built in 1809), which signaled the beginning of the Industrial Revolution in the state. Brunswick also prides itself on to Bowdoin College, a small private institution incorporated in 1794. On the campus and nearby, the famous Bowdoin Pines—regal, tall white pines—hint at what must have covered much of southern Maine prior to the advent of logging. Surprising to most people, the pines

are actually younger than the college itself. With its mills and the steady employment provided by the college, Brunswick grew to be a community of nearly 20,000—the largest along the entire Mid-coast region.

Brunswick seems an unlikely place to spawn a major anti-slavery book, but Harriett Beecher Stowe, the wife of a young Bowdoin professor, Calvin Stowe, had a vision during a Brunswick church service in 1851. In her vision, an old black slave, Tom, was unmercifully flogged to death by Simon Legree, the cruel overseer, and two other slaves. Stowe wrote down the vision, which provided inspiration for her novel *Uncle Tom's Cabin*, a book that heightened awareness of the inhumanity of slavery. *Uncle Tom's Cabin* sold 305,000 copies its first year alone! Many believe Stowe's book helped spur the North to war over the slavery issue.

Just up the coast from Brunswick, Bath musters 10,000 people, or about half the population of Brunswick, and ranks the as second-largest Mid-coast community. If Brunswick exudes an intellectual air as a result of Bowdoin College, Bath is definitely a working town, well known as the home for Bath Iron Works, Maine's large private employer. More than 10,000 at BIW construct ships for the navy and merchant marine. Bath's first commercial shipyard opened in 1762, and by the mid-1800s more than 200 ship-building firms along the Kennebec River produced more than half the nation's sailing vessels. Between 1862 and 1902, Bath was the fifth-largest seaport in the nation.

South of Bath, two of Maine's most undeveloped and beautiful sand beaches lie on opposite sides of the Morse River: Seawall Beach, owned by the Nature Conservancy, and Popham Beach at Popham Beach State Park.

Seawall Beach provides one of the best undeveloped examples of a barrier spit left in the state. At low tide the beach, nearly 400 feet wide, complements the largest parabolic dune field complex in Maine.

A number of plants reach their northernmost ranges here, including beach heather, with 90 percent of the known population in Maine found here. The northernmost population of the earthstar puffball also occurs in this location. In addition, Seawall Beach offers one of the few nesting sites for piping plovers and least terns in Maine—both endangered species, existing here at the northern edges of their ranges.

Popham Beach, too, is among the widest beaches in the state. Unlike most sand beaches in Maine, which derive their sands from reworked glacial till, Popham Beach receives sand from the nearby Kennebec River. One of the interesting features of Popham Beach is the Fox Island Tombolo. A tombolo is a sandbar that connects two islands to each other, or an island to the mainland. At all but high tide, visitors can walk the tombolo out to the island.

Behind the Popham Beach dunes and along the Morse River lies Popham Marsh. The most abundant plants in the marsh are appropriately named saltgrasses—salt-marsh cordgrass and salt-meadow cordgrass. Salt-marsh cordgrass, the taller of the two, tolerates flooding better and grows along the wettest parts of the marsh,

Above: Bath Iron Works—the largest employer in the state of Maine. More people work here than in the entire Maine fishing industry.
Facing page: Autumn color at the Bowdoin College campus in Brunswick, a major textile mill center during the Industrial Revolution.

slows evaporation, roots that tolerate low oxygen and frequent flooding, and an ability to excrete excess salt from their leaves.

On the uplands surrounding the marsh, and on older nearby dunes beyond the reach of most salt spray, grows pitch pine, a shrubby tree with short needles. Pitch pine is fire-adapted to quickly recolonize burned sites, an advantage in competition with other trees. However, on nutrient-poor sites like sand dunes, pitch pine encounters little competition and can maintain itself for long intervals without fires.

The next river beyond the Kennebec and Popham Beach, the Sheepscot, forms one of Maine's finest harbors near its mouth—Boothbay Harbor. Sheepscot originally supported one of the largest fishing fleets on the Maine coast, but fishing largely has yielded to fleets of yachts and tourist shops. For those who like to shop in a nice setting, Boothbay is the place to stay. But as one local wryly told me, "the only good thing about Boothbay is that it's not far from the Maine coast." What he meant, of course, is that Boothbay Harbor is more or less dominated by antique and gift shops, and to see working fishing villages requires going a little farther afield. Fifty tour boats operate in summer from Boothbay Harbor, so there's plenty of opportunity for visitors to extend their circles of exploration.

Two of the more interesting coastal areas accessible from Boothbay are Monhegan Island and Damariscove Island. Monhegan, 10 miles off the coast, was described by Captain John Smith, who landed with a crew in 1614. Some of his men camped here to catch and dry cod. When they returned to Europe with their booty, they put Monhegan on the map. Accounts of the island's attractions may have led to its first fishing station in 1625 and permanent settlement since 1674.

Monhegan had 65 year-round residents in 1960 and 120 in 1986, crucial numbers to island dwellers. The loss of

while the shorter salt-meadow grass inhabits drier areas that only occasionally flood. In the past, farmers harvested saltgrasses for cattle forage.

Both plants developed unusual adaptations to survive in the briny tidal environment, including tolerance for high salt concentrations in their cells, a thick cuticle or skin that

one or two families, especially those with children, may mean the local school will close. In 1984, eight children attended Monhegan's one-room school house—the bare minimum. Without a school, other families may move away and older people dependent upon them will go, too.

The central building on Monhegan is the old lighthouse. Built in 1822, the light was automated in 1959. When the Coast Guard sold the building in 1962, it was bought by Monhegan Associates, a group of citizens organized to preserve the historic and natural features of the island. Gradually, they transformed the lighthouse buildings into a museum on island history and the islanders' way of life.

Today, Monhegan is a favorite for summer residents, particularly artists. Its dramatic scenery has inspired such artists as Rockwell Kent, Jamie Wyeth and Charles Martin.

Tourists in ever-greater numbers also find Monhegan inspiring. Most people walk, since Monhegan prohibits vehicles except for hauling heavy equipment or gear. Almost all travel here is by bike or hiking the excellent trail system that extends to the far corners of the island. And there is much to see from these trails, including some of the largest cliffs on the Maine coast—where gulls swirl above pounding surf.

Damariscove Island was the site of the earliest fishing station in Maine, where fishermen established a year-round station in 1622. Sheep grazing began in the mid-1700s and dairy cows were added later. A fire in 1890 destroyed Damariscove's limited timber and today the narrow island is entirely treeless. In 1896, the Coast Guard built a Life Saving Station that was manned year-round, and the population grew to 30 residents. However, by 1939, its year-round residents abandoned the island for the mainland and by 1959 the Coast Guard moved also. In 1966 the Nature Conservancy obtained the island. Today Damaris-

cove is one of the outstanding bird-nesting areas of the entire coast.

Up the coast from Boothbay Harbor, beyond the Damariscotta River and Johns Bay, Pemaquid Point features one of the most stunning and picturesque lighthouses on the entire coast of Maine. Built in 1827, the Pemaquid Point Lighthouse was automated in 1934. Beyond the lighthouse, the point itself alternates layers of dark schists and lighter quartzites, now tilted on edge and weathered in bands. These metamorphic rocks originally derived from ocean-bottom sediments. Softer rock eroded away faster than harder rock, resulting in the grooves so prominent here.

The next major headland up the coast, Marshall Point near the pretty fishing village of Port Clyde, consists of rock entirely different from that of Pemaquid Point.

Above: Yachting near Monhegan Island
Facing page: Monhegan Island. Site of one of the earliest fishing stations on the entire Maine coast. Fishermen were using Monhegan as a base of operation as early as the 1620s.

With the protection of the Penobscot Bay Islands, the bay itself has become the East Coast's center for yachting and sailing.

Left: Lighthouse at Pemaquid Point
Facing page: Surf at sunset, Pemaquid Point.

Marshall Point, made of granite, has weathered into huge blocks.

As you round Marshall Point and pass through Two Bush Channel, you enter Penobscot Bay. The bay, the largest on the Maine coast, measures 30 miles wide by 30 miles long and sports islands of every size, including several large ones such as Vinalhaven, North Haven and Isleboro. Although much of the bay's southwest coast is metamorphic rock, many of the islands are composed primarily of granitic rocks. Unlike the metamorphic-rock islands that dominate farther west, these granitic islands tend to be rounder and blockier.

Quarrying once fueled a major enterprise along the Maine coast from Port Clyde to Mount Desert Island, with Penobscot Bay as its center. Spruce Head, Vinalhaven and Hurricane islands, among other Penobscot Bay islands, furnished important sources of granite for buildings all along the Eastern coast of the United States.

Although pieces of the Penobscot Bay islands once were slowly carted away to construct city buildings, today

Above: Known for its quaint setting, Rockport originally was a major shipping port for lime made from local limestone.
Right: View of Penobscot Bay and Camden from Camden Hills State Park. Penobscot Bay is the largest bay on the coast of Maine.
Facing page: Early morning in Camden Boat Harbor. Camden is a favorite port of call for yachts.

these islands are more valuable in place. They offer protection from the force of the open ocean, making Penobscot Bay the center for yachting and sailing on the entire coast. Prior to the American Revolution, this bay formed a major natural line between various warring factions. Even today, Mainers accept it as the boundary between Mid-coast and Downeast.

A number of important communities line the 30-mile length of Penobscot Bay's southwestern coast, including Rockland Harbor. Rockland—with 8,400 people—is the largest community on Penobscot Bay and one of Maine's largest fishing ports in terms of volume and value of catch processed. The harbor also features several state-owned ferries that serve Matinicus, Vinalhaven and North Haven islands. Rockland's name refers to its past prominence as a lime-processing center. Lime was used for mortar and plaster, providing one of Rockland's major industries. As early as 1730, residents pioneered liming in the area and by 1785 they had built lime kilns on Rockland harbor, from which they shipped the lime. Abandoned lime kilns still line the shore.

Not to be confused with Rockland is Rockport. While Rockland operates as a working harbor, Rockport's lovely harbor relies on recreation and tourism. Like Rockland, Rockport once depended upon liming and ship building for its livelihood, but when these commercial enterprises began to die out around the turn of the century, tourists and summer residents discovered Rockport. Today it is well known for its cultural attributes, which include the Maine Photography workshops, Bay Chamber Music series and the preservation of boat-building skills by the Rockport Apprenticeship Program.

Rockport and Camden, separated by a few miles of highway, have much in common. Camden, one of the major communities along the Mid-coast with a population of 4,650, devotes itself largely to tourism and yachting. The spectacular Camden Harbor, backed by the 1,400-foot Camden Hills, part of Camden Hills State Park, usually fills in summer with yachts and schooners acting as cruise ships. Many of the old, large, restored houses dating from Camden's heyday as a seaport and shipping center give the town an air of aristocratic wealth not found in many other coastal towns.

Near the head of Penobscot Bay lies Searsport, Maine's second-largest deepwater seaport. Searsport boasts a long maritime tradition that produced 250 large sailing vessels and 286 sea captains. During the late 1800s, 10 percent of the nation's merchant-marine sea captains called Searsport home. Elegant, spacious homes overlooking the bay recall this era of relative wealth and prosperity. Today, Searsport appears to be the "antique capital" of Maine, with more than 20 shops.

The Mid-coast encompasses, for many people, the "real" Maine. From tiny fishing villages to larger communities like Brunswick and Camden, the mid-coast is the Maine coast as visitors expect it.

LOBSTERS

Although finned fish may be important commercially to Maine's fishing industry, lobstering and lobsters are strongly associated with the state's image. Lobster fishing not only contributes to the aesthetic appeal of the coast, but also supplied $54.5 million income to lobster fishermen in 1987. Without lobstering and the income it provides, many coastal villages would empty.

Americans did not always consider lobsters choice fare. Lobsters once so abounded along the Maine coast that Mainers could capture them from tidepools, or regularly catch large individuals four feet long and weighing up to 50 pounds. These common creatures were considered "trash food" to be eaten only in times of scar-

city. An old Maine law even stated that prisoners could not be fed lobster more than twice a week, for to do so was inhumane treatment.

Lobsters are crustaceans, or shellfish, that feed primarily at night. Their natural distribution extends from North Carolina to Labrador. Because the lobster must molt its outside skeleton—called an exoskeleton—to grow, growth is relatively slow and five to six years pass in the cold Maine waters before these crustaceans reach sexual maturity. Its slow sexual development limits the lobster fishing

industry. Some evidence suggests that fishermen already are straining the lobster's natural potential to reproduce.

In recent years, lobster fishermen also have suffered the spiraling escalation of costs and effort. In the past, a lobsterman built his own boat of wood. He constructed traps from wood during the slack time of year. He hauled traps up by hand, and no one used radar. Under such conditions, a fisherman could reasonably put out only a hundred traps.

However, in the 1960s, lobster fishing underwent dramatic changes. It be-

came more sophisticated and, unfortunately for the fisherman, more expensive. Hydraulic equipment enabled one man to work his boat and load many more traps in a single day. Hauling up more traps required placing them over greater distances, and the old outboard motors and skiffs gave way to larger diesel-powered boats. Radar, although it increased safety in fog, also increased costs. Wire traps, introduced widely in the late 1970s, lasted longer than the old wooden traps and required less tending, but they, too, cost more.

Since the expense of

outfitting a modern boat considerably exceeded the amount necessary to operate the old skiff-and-wooden-trap way, fishermen borrowed heavily. Interest and insurance payments ate up a substantial portion of a fisherman's income. In order to pay these loans, fishermen had to set out more traps and burn more gasoline. By the mid-1980s, many lobster fishermen were putting out as many as 600 or more traps. Yet their catches remained relatively stable as the number of lobster caught per trap declined. Lobstermen were definitely in a bind.

Statistics compiled by the Department of Marine Resources document this trend. In 1892, 2,600 people in the lobster business used small boats and—by today's standards—primitive equipment, yet they needed only 109,000 traps to land

17.6 million pounds of lobster. In 1958, 6,236 fishermen used 550,000 lobster traps to increase their catch to 25 million pounds. However, by 1965, the number of fishermen had decreased slightly to 5,800, but traps had increased to 789,000. Only 17 million pounds of lobster were taken—the same as in 1892 with only 109,000 traps. Ten years later, in 1975, traps numbered 1,700,000, but the catch had decreased even further to 15.4 million pounds. By 1982 there were 8,895 lobster fishermen setting out more than 2 million traps, almost 20 times the number reported in 1892, yet the catch barely improved to 20.7 million pounds.

Recently, Mainers have made several attempts to limit trap numbers—at least locally. In 1984, the fishermen on Swans Island, for example, enacted

a local trap limit of 500 traps for a single fishermen and 600 traps for a boat with two people working it. The ordinance gradually reduces the trap limit to 300 and 400 traps, respectively, by 1990. Despite immense initial resistance, the limits seem to be working as intended. The 1986 and 1987 seasons were two of the best in recent memory and support for the program increased. However, trap limits may invite more people to set traps, thereby negating the value of limitations.

Limited entry quotas discourage increasing numbers of fishermen. Under such quotas, only fishermen who currently fish can continue fishing. Anyone else must buy the permit of another fisherman. Obviously, this system—already implemented in Alaska's salmon fisheries—gives proprietary rights to individuals for a public resource—the fisheries. Thus, access becomes private property. In addition, opponents charge that quota systems would make fishing even more expensive, since the cost of a permit could spiral upwards, as occurred in Alaska, until it costs more than a boat or equipment. Quotas might make lobster fishing financially impossible for many Maine coastal residents.

Trap limits and entry quotas are only two means of dealing with a declining fishery. Maine set a size limit designed to protect lobster breeding stock. However, studies have shown that the size limitation may prove ineffective, since as many as 80 percent of harvested female lobsters have not reached breeding age. In recent years, fishing pressure has been so intense that nearly all lobsters are harvested as soon as they reach legal

size, hence most reproduction may be by a very small percentage of the population. In an effort to increase the population of breeding adults, the legal size is being increased.

Although a size limit can improve lobster numbers, it does have a cost. With the requirement to throw back smaller lobsters, many young lobsters are injured or even eaten by larger ones while temporarily in the traps. In addition, as fishermen haul lobsters up and handle them on boats, short lobsters often are hurt or damaged, losing legs, antennae and other body parts. Thus, even though they are returned to the sea, they often die or grow very slowly because of their handicaps. Future lobster harvests suffer.

The lobster may be a symbol of the Maine coast, but apparently—as with nearly every natural re-

source—we must over-exploit it before we decide to conserve it. The lobster industry faces serious trouble and only strong conservation measures can ensure its survival: perhaps special marine wilderness preserves prohibiting lobster or other commercial fishing along coastal areas off Acadia National Park,

and wildlife refuges like Petit Manan, could be placed off-limits to commercial fishing, just as we set aside wilderness areas on land to preserve terrestrial ecosystems. These areas would provide scientific "control" populations for marine research as well as genetic reservoirs.

Above: A lobster house at Stonington.
Facing page: Lobster Traps at Islesford, Little Cranberry Island.

Downeast
CHAPTER 7

*T*he Downeast Coast is closer to the rising sun than any other piece of continental U.S. real estate. Sailors adopted the name "downeast" during the early years of settlement, when ships left Boston bound for the Maine coast with the southwest wind filling their sails and their bows pointed to the east, hence going downwind while heading east. The residents of this then-lonely stretch of the North American frontier became known as "Downeasters."

For the purposes of this book, the Downeast Coast includes all the Maine coastline between the mill town of Bucksport at the upper end of Penobscot Bay, eastward to Passamaquoddy Bay near the fishing village of Lubec. It includes one of the coastal region's main tourist attractions—Acadia National Park—as well as some of the most remote portions of the coast. Washington County's largest community, Calais, has only 4,050 residents.

Downeast Maine epitomizes rocky coast. Granite headlands and islands make up much of the rugged strand with Deer Isle, Mount Desert Island, the Schoodic Peninsula and Great Wass Island some of the more prominent granite outcrops. East of Great Wass, Maine's coast exhibits no more exposed granite outcrops. Except for the mountains on Mount Desert Island, most of this coast features low relief.

Rocky headlands abound, and there are few beaches. The hard granite that dominates so much of the coast has had little time to erode since the last Ice Age and, consequently, there is little sediment for sandy beaches. With the exceptions of Rogue Beach by Englishman Bay and Sand Beach at Acadia National Park, almost no significant sandy beaches punctuate this entire stretch of coast.

Right: Early morning at Whiting Narrows on Cobscook Bay. The undeveloped nature of Cobscook Bay and the Bold Coast make this region desirable for potential public acquisition. There has been discussion of a new "Bold Coast" national park.
Facing page: Early morning on Long Pond, Acadia National Park. Most of the freshwater lakes in the park were carved by glaciers.

Small, rocky islands pepper large bays such as Englishman, Machias, Blue Hill, Narraguagus and the northeast shore of Penobscot Bay. Yet, east of Machias Bay deep bays and islands give way to what is sometimes called the "bold" coast. Its relatively straight, cliff-strewn face resulted from shearing of the earth's crust along the Fundy Fault. However, Cobscook Bay by Lubec marks a further change in the land's character. The straight coast gives way to a system of peninsulas separated by bays.

Because of the narrow constrictions between these long arms of the sea, this area records the greatest tidal amplitude in the U.S.—outside Alaska—with spring tides often exceeding 24 feet. Turbulent tides and whirlpools stir up nutrients, and thus, biologically, this is one of the richest parts of the coast. Abundant fish feed the largest U.S. coastal assemblage of Bonaparte's gulls, herring gulls and black-legged kittiwakes as well as the highest concentration of nesting bald eagles in the Northeast.

The northern Gulf of Maine and Bay of Fundy contain waters that are both nutritionally richer and cooler than those to the south. Cool water meeting the air results in more fog and precipitation, particularly in summer. This region owns the dubious distinction of having the coolest and wettest summers of any location on the entire Eastern Seaboard.

Although not exactly ideal for sun bathers and beach combers, the wet, cool, foggy climate ideally suits spruce and fir forests, which give the region a distinctly northern character. Many of these trees—particularly those found on the wetter, cooler outer islands and headlands—are

Early snowfall covers hills by Northeast Harbor, Mount Desert Island. Northeast Harbor is one of the communities, like Bar Harbor, that became popular with wealthy "summer people" during the late 1800s and early 1900s. The lovely large homes that are sometimes called "cottages" are one of the attractions of this region.

ally acquire elevated, dome-like surfaces. Several species of plants uncommon in Maine inhabit these coastal bogs, including cloudberry—a plant common in Alaska and across Canada. More accessible coastal raised peat bogs include Carrying Place Cove Bog by Lubec and Big Heath in Acadia National Park.

Neither climate or vegetation first attracted European people to this coast, but rather the bounty of the sea, and the region's strategic location between lands claimed by France and those under English domination. One of the most fought-over sites, the village of Castine, changed flags nine times between its settlement in 1630—as a trading outpost for Massachusetts' Plymouth Rock Company—and the end of the War of 1812. The quiet, shaded streets lined with elegant homes belie the turbulence of Castine's early history, when the French, Dutch, English and Americans alternately occupied the village. One of the costliest naval battles of the entire Revolution occurred here, when the patriots lost nearly their entire attacking fleet of 44 vessels as well as 500 lives while dislodging the British from Fort George, now a historic site.

To the south of Castine lie Deer Isle and Stonington. Castine existed for nearly 150 years before Stonington was founded. Stonington, as its name implies, once was a center for Maine's granite quarry industry. Even today, a distinctive feature of Stonington's harbor is the granite construction of the many wharves and docks. Stonington is what Boothbay Harbor claims to be, and what many other coastal towns like Rockport and Bar Harbor might like to be—an authentic Maine fishing village. Commercial fishing boats, not yachts, crowd the harbor, and an assortment of baitshacks and boatyards, plus a packing plant, surrounds the working harbor. Clean, well kept houses perch on a nearby hill.

Although commercial fishing sustains the economy today, granite led to the town's establishment. Stone from nearby quarries helped construct Rockefeller Center in New

richly draped with epiphytic lichens, presenting shaggy, bedraggled appearances.

Another indicator of northerly climatic conditions is jack pine, a species common in the Great Lakes region but rare in Maine. On cool, wet headlands and outer islands, the red-barked jack pine grows amid soft white "caribou moss." Jack pine reaches its southern range limit on Mount Desert Island.

A vegetational-geological feature rare elsewhere on the Maine coast, but relatively common on the Downeast coast, is the raised peat bog. Such bogs maintain their own water tables, unrelated to nearby groundwater, and gradu-

Stonington is what some coastal towns claim to be, and what others might wish to be—a working fishing village.

Sardine cannery at Lubec. The sardine fishery was once a major industry in the Cobscook Bay region—Eastport alone once boasted 68 canneries.

Railroads made the granite of Maine's quarries available for 19th-century buildings throughout the Northeast.

lieve Isle au Haut is the most beautiful part of the entire park. In the 1800s the island claimed 274 residents, mostly fishermen and their families, but mainland conveniences gradually siphoned away population, and today no more than 70 year-round residents call Isle au Haut home.

Although millions throng to the main portion of Acadia, only 50 people a day are allowed to visit Isle au Haut. Access is primarily by mailboat and tourboat, and the island contains no accommodations other than a single National Park Service campground. Most visitors stay only six hours before catching the mailboat back to Stonington.

Somewhat hilly, Isle au Haut stands out in Penobscot Bay because of 556-foot Mt. Champlain, the tallest peak on any Maine island except Mount Desert Island. But hills are only part of the romance of Isle au Haut, for the island also features nearly-untrod rocky beaches, lonely lakes and undisturbed woods.

On the mainland beyond Stonington, Blue Hill was named for a 500-foot promontory visible from the higher mountains in Acadia National Park as well as other parts of the coast. The hill, covered with blueberry barrens, provides a

York, the U.S. Naval Academy in Annapolis and the Museum of Fine Arts in Boston. When the building trades turned to concrete instead of granite, most of the local quarries closed. Granite still is quarried on nearby Crotch Island, but fewer than a dozen workers are employed there.

Eight miles south of Stonington, beyond the fragmented maze of small islands known as Merchant Row, lies the wild Isle au Haut. Some 2,860 acres of the 5,500-acre island belong to Acadia National Park and many people be-

magnificent view of Blue Hill Bay and the surrounding mainland. The town of Blue Hill is especially significant because the entire community is listed as a National Historic District.

Unlike many of the villages lining this section of the coast, Blue Hill did not originate as a fishing center. Rather, it began with the lumber trade and a sawmill constructed in 1765. Ship building followed the lumber industry, and boosted Blue Hill's economy for almost a century. But perhaps the most unusual aspect of Blue Hill is its brief history as a mining town. Copper was discovered here in 1876 and the community boomed until copper prices crashed five years later.

Travelers wending their way from Blue Hill toward Mount Desert Island and Acadia National Park pass through Ellsworth, the commercial hub of the Downeast Coast. The main highway in Ellsworth leading to Acadia National Park reflects the future that threatens Maine's coast—a strip of undistinctive malls, fast-food restaurants and gas stations. Ellsworth counts 93 square miles within its city limits—the largest area of any Maine city.

South toward Acadia, the strip development crowds the highway with factory outlets, trinket stores and other tourist establishments. However, such development stops with Mount Desert Island itself and, once inside the borders of Acadia National Park, visitors see careful development harmonizing with natural beauty. The telephone poles, neon signs and parking lots give way to pleasant woodlands laced by carriage trails and beautiful ocean-front drives. Acadia, the only coastal national park north of Florida, boasts the highest eastern coastal mountains outside Canada.

As the largest coastal island in Maine, Mount Desert offers more than spectacular Acadia National Park alone. Prior to the 1840s, Bar Harbor was a small fishing village.

Above: Blueberry barren at Englishman Bay southest of Jonesboro. Washington County is the nation's leader in wild blueberry production. **Facing page:** Bass Harbor Lighthouse—one of the most famous lighthouses on the entire Maine coast—on Mount Desert Island.

Then in 1844, Thomas Cole, one of the famous painters of the Hudson River School, spent part of the summer on a farm by Schooner Head. His paintings of the Maine coast drew other artists to the region, and their wealthy patrons—the "rusticators"—soon followed. Artists and rusticators alike boarded with local farmers and fishermen. Then in the 1880s through the 1920s, Mt. Desert Island and Bar Harbor came of age as the premier vacation spot for the East Coast's wealthy upper crust, who built lavish summer homes modestly called "cottages." This gilded age lasted nearly 50 years until the stock market crash of 1929 brought an abrupt end to many family fortunes.

Although past wealth still permeates the many mansions and large old houses that dominate Bar Harbor, a surprising number of ordinary working villages dot Northeast Harbor and other portions of Mount Desert Island. Bass Harbor, a picturesque fishing village on the southwest

corner of the island, presents one of the most photographed lighthouses on the entire Maine coast.

However, to glimpse Maine coast villages less altered by time, abandon Mount Desert altogether and venture by ferry to one of the offshore island communities like Swans Island, Long Island (Frenchboro) or the Cranberry Islands. Here, insulated by the surrounding water, the pace of life is slower and the popular image of hard-working fishermen and their families wresting a living from the sea is not yet outdated. Islanders use the roads as sidewalks because auto traffic is so light. Bicycles offer an ideal way to explore these islands.

Across Frenchman Bay and farther up the coast, is Washington County, sometimes touted by tourist promotions as Sunrise County because it is the first place in the U.S. to greet the new day. Numerous bays, points and headlands resemble those of the Mid-coast, but the bays are wider, points blunter and channels broader. However, bays like Pleasant, Machias, Englishman and Cobscook shelter many working fishing villages that are the most isolated, and thus unchanged, on the entire Maine coast. Not surprisingly, this least "touristy" portion of Maine's coast is also the poorest.

The area around Milbridge and Cherryfield on the Narraguagus River is renowned for its blueberry production and Cherryfield claims to be the "Blueberry Capital of the World." Indeed, 200,000 acres of blueberry barrens in Washington County produce 90 percent of the nation's wild blueberry crop. The plants take on a rich red color with autumn, and the barrens add a beautiful foliage and texture to the landscape.

Every two years, growers burn their blueberry fields to stimulate growth of new berry plants. A burned field does not produce berries until the following August, when workers scoop up ripening berries with dustpan shaped rakes.

Up the coast and near the outer fringes of land lie the communities of Jonesport and Beals. The two communities, separated by a bridge over Mooseabec Reach, claim the largest lobster fleet north of Penobscot Bay. However, clams also are commercially important, and Beals Island is home to the Regional Shellfish Hatchery, which raised 8 million clams in 1987 and planted some 3 million of them in nearby mud flats. Washington County mud flats provide 45 percent of Maine's clam production.

Beyond Beals, Great Wass Island reaches farther into the Gulf of Maine than any other part of Washington County. A good proportion of Great Wass Island is a Nature Conservancy preserve. Because it reaches so far out into the Gulf of Maine, Great Wass Island experiences greater wind, precipitation and fog, and cooler temperatures, than nearby mainland areas. Consequently, a distinctly subarctic "feel" characterizes vegetation here. For example, one of the largest stands of jack pine in the state grows here, close to a number of raised coastal peatlands—both more common in Canada's Maritime Provinces.

At the head of Machias Bay lie the tri-communities of Machias, Machiasport and East Machias, which share a great deal of Maine's early history. Although explored early in the 1600s, conflicting sovereignty claims and Indian attacks postponed permanent settlement of this portion of Maine until 1763. When Machias gained township status in 1770, it became the first permanent town east of the Penobscot River.

Shortly after gaining status as a town, Machias played a role in the American Revolution. When a Machias Loyalist brought not only British goods from Boston to sell, but also an armed British schooner for enforcement, Machias residents called a meeting in the Burnham Tavern, which still stands. Fueled by anger, and no doubt alcohol, the rebels brashly decided to capture the schooner, *Margaretta*. Luck was with the Americans and, after two of their ships chased the *Margaretta* down the Machias River, they captured it, ending the first naval battle of the revolution.

Left: A foggy day in Cutler.
Facing page: Whiting Bay on Cobscook Bay, Cobscook Bay State Park.

The nearby town of Machiasport preserves the scant remains of Fort O'Brien, hastily constructed after the *Margaretta* episode to protect Machias from retaliation (which the British intended but never were able to attempt). During the War of 1812, the British sacked the fort, but it was rebuilt and re-armed during the Civil War. Today nothing much remains of one of the major military defense posts on the Maine coast, except some low mounds and a few cannons.

After the Revolution the tri-towns of Machias, East Machias and Machiasport became important lumber milling sites and shipping ports for wood exports, especially after the towns became the terminus of the Machias-Whitneyville railroad. Ship building was another prominent local trade.

Just east of Machias, the Little River slips past the tranquil fishing hamlet of Cutler. Cutler's lifeblood is the sea, particularly lobster trapping. Concerned about depleting stocks, the community opened a lobster hatchery in 1988. Fertilized eggs stripped from female lobsters hatch into young that feed on tiny brine shrimp raised by hatchery personnel. In its first year, the hatchery released 20,000 lobsters into the wild, and production subsequently increased.

From Cutler to Cobscook Bay stretches the nearly straight "Bold Coast"—the result of a break in the earth's crust along the Fundy Fault. Most of the land along this isolated strand remains undeveloped—the least populated, most remote and, some would say, most spectacular section of the entire Maine coast. The area's superb qualities were recognized when the state of Maine Critical Areas Program nominated Bold Coast as a federal National Natural Landmark. However, designation as a National Natural Landmark does not in and of itself guarantee any legal protection for the area's superb qualities.

But the coastline's magnificent features attracted national attention, too. In 1988, the National Parks and Con-

servation Association, a private organization, included the Bold Coast and Cobscook Bay among 68 areas of the country it thought worthy of national park status and protection. According to the NPCA report, the "Bold Coast is basically the last undeveloped coastal area in Maine. It is spectacular—rocky crags meet the fury of the sea—and of great ecological diversity...The stretch of coast north of Cutler may be the last opportunity to set aside additional portions of this dramatic land and sea-scape before mankind irreversibly alters it."

This portion of Washington County undoubtedly contains some of the most scenic coastline in Maine. However, many local residents reject the park proposal. Locals usually want to keep things "just the way they are." Nevertheless, things have not been very good here of late. Employment in the twin pillars of Washington County's economic base—the wood products and fishing industries—has declined. Many local residents fondly remember the "good old days" when a high school graduate could find high-paying jobs that required little training or formal education. Large development schemes became particularly attractive. As early as the 1930s, massive plans for local employment proposed harnessing the huge tides of Passamaquoddy Bay by constructing a giant electrical generation plant. More recently, there was serious discussion of constructing a major oil refinery near Eastport.

Washington County has seen hard times in recent years. Eastport, the easternmost city in the country and the northernmost city on the U.S. Eastern Seaboard, reflects the country at large. Once home to 6,000 residents at the turn of the century, Eastport saw population drop to 2,500 by 1960 and to only 1,900 by 1986. Some locals joke about Eastport's greatest export: "high school graduates."

But Eastport is smiling these days. Modest house prices have attracted new year-round and summer residents. Ocean Products, an aquaculture venture that raises Atlantic salmon

Washington County calls itself "Sunrise County" because it is the first place in the continental U.S. to greet the new day.

Left: Fog surrounds spruce at Quoddy Head Bog in Quoddy Head State Park.
Facing page: Cliffs at Buckman Head on Passamaquoddy Bay near Eastport. The tidal amplitude in Passamaquoddy Bay, a tributary of the Bay of Fundy, is the highest in Maine. The area has been considered a prime location for tidal electrical energy generation.

for harvest, has grown rapidly. And Eastport's ice-free port has helped sustain its shipping industry.

Nevertheless, tourism probably offers the most regional growth in terms of employment. The location of Eastport and other communities in Washington County, just across the bay from Roosevelt Campobello Island In-ternational Park in New Brunswick, plus the scenic attractions of Moosehorn National Wildlife Refuge and Cobscook Bay, should ensure a growing share of the tourist dollar. Washington County will not remain undeveloped forever.

ACADIA NATIONAL PARK

Acadia National Park is located on Mount Desert Island, the largest coastal island in Maine. The waters of Frenchman Bay define its northern shore and Blue Hill Bay lies to the south. Somes Sound, a glacial fiord, nearly splits the island in two.

Much of the park's natural beauty results from its geological history. Granite, formed deep in the earth, accounts for most of the exposed rock surfaces. Glaciers smoothed off mountains and gouged out lakes and U-shaped valleys. The park also includes Cadillac Mountain, 1,530 feet in elevation—the highest coastal mountain on the Downeast coast.

A lush and varied vegetative cover contrasts with the bare rock. Near the headlands and outer coast, a lichen-encrusted spruce-fir forest dominates. Inland, hardwoods such as birch and aspen become more common, especially in the eastern portion of the park where the 1947 forest fire burned much of the landscape.

In his 1604 logs, French explorer Samuel Champlain described an island with very high mountains whose summits were barren of trees, which he named "Isle des Monts-deserts." More than 300 years later, this island of bare rock has become one of the most popular national parks in the country.

Except for one short-lived French settlement at Fernald Point on Somes Sound abandoned in 1613, permanent settlement on Mount Desert Island did not come until the mid-1700s. By the mid-

1800s, several fishing villages dotted the island, and farms covered many of the flatter coastal real estate.

Beginning around 1840, the magnificent scenery began to attract a seasonal clientele, mostly urban high-society types, who spent their summers vacationing in Maine. By 1880, dozens of hotels served these visitors and the wealthy began to build their "cottages."

Disturbed that development might overwhelm the island's quiet beauty, some of its wealthy residents formed the Hancock County Trustees of Public Reservations in 1901 to buy some of the island's most scenic features and preserve them for future generations. By 1913, the trustees had acquired more than 5,000 acres, including the summit of Cadillac Mountain. In 1916, the same year the National Park Service was created,

Low tide at Stonington

ship. In 1919, a name change made it Lafayette National Park, the first national park east of the Mississippi River. In 1929, a donation of the Schoodic Peninsula expanded the park and its name became Acadia.

Unlike most national parks created from existing public lands, Acadia resulted largely from the generous donations of wealthy landholders. One of the major contributors to Acadia National Park's expansion, John D. Rockefeller, Jr., donated more than 10,700 acres to Acadia—more than a third of the park. Rockefeller also built 51 miles of carriage roads that lace the park and now are used as bike, hiking and horse riding trails, providing a tranquil pathway for today's visitors.

Today, Acadia encompasses 35,057 acres of the Maine coast including two separate units: 2,000 acres

the trustees donated their holdings to the United States. President Woodrow Wilson accepted the lands by proclaiming the establishment of Sieur de Monts National Monument. Sieur de Monts had captained Champlain's

on the Schoodic Peninsula and 3,000 acres on Isle Au Haut or "high island." Recent legislation strongly supported by local citizens fixed a permanent boundary around the park to prevent any further expansion. The law even prohibits donations, although limited funds have been appropriated for the purchase of private inholdings. However, this $7 million will—given the high land values along coastal Maine and on Mount Desert Island in particular—buy very little new parkland.

The restriction on boundary expansions will make future management exceedingly difficult. The present park, a patchwork of private and public lands, makes cohesive management impossible. In addition, Acadia encompasses only parts of many important parcels of wildlife habitat, vegetative communities and watersheds.

Moreover, the park's present boundaries unfortunately do not protect the offshore marine environment. Although it might be unpopular with local fishermen, it could be argued that, from an aesthetic point of view, some portion of the coast, perhaps a quarter mile offshore along Acadia's borders, should be closed to all forms of commercial fishing. Yet such a closure seems justified by science as well. There is absolutely no scientific control area on the Maine coast prohibiting human exploitation of fisheries, and such an area could provide invaluable comparisons with exploited populations. We might once again find lobsters four feet long in the waters around Mount Desert Island—as Mainers found in the days before heavy commercial fishing.

Parks do not exist as isolated landscapes, not

even island parks. According to a recent Harvard University study, encroaching development threatens Acadia's "unique character if not its very survival." Visitation is crushing the park. In 1987 more than 4.3 million people visited Acadia, making it the second-most-popular national park in the country. On an average summer day, 4,000 cars will drive Ocean Drive, the park's most popular road.

Most local businesses, although they support limiting expansion of the park, oppose limits upon themselves. Roadside development along the Route 3 corridor to Acadia compromises the beauty of the park's main highway. Overnight units in Bar Harbor, for example, increased from 1,500 to 2,256 between 1983 and 1986. And some park officials contend that conges-tion can be controlled only if nearby towns limit development.

Air pollution ignores political boundaries. The highest ozone levels ever recorded in Maine occurred on Isle au Haut in June 1988. Smog reduces scenic vistas, of course, but it also physically endangers humans. The same dirty air is killing spruce and has noticeably harmed 58 percent of the park's white pine. Carried by prevailing winds, smog comes primarily from the Boston—New York—Washington megalopolis.

Funding plagues Acadia. The park's $1.9 million annual budget does not cover upkeep, much less resource protection and inventory. The park, for example, has never even compiled a thorough list of its fauna and flora. A frustrated ranger confided his exasperation to me: "How can we protect

something if we don't know what's there and how many there are to begin with?"

Given the limited publicly accessible acreage on Maine's entire coast, why restrict potential expansion of the park? Acadia represents the largest single tract of publicly accessible, publicly owned real estate on the Maine coast, yet it protects a pitifully small amount of land. New York's 6-million-acre Adirondack State Park, by comparison, is nearly 20 times the size of Acadia.

Will Acadia survive into the 21st century as a beautiful example of the Maine coast or become just another overgrown natural amusement park? The answer depends greatly on how park and local officials cope with rising visitation and development beyond the park borders. Acadia will reflect how well we recognize that the park, like the earth, has finite limits. Once, the entire planet was a "park." Today, even the last small vestiges of our pristine earth seem threatened by contamination. The choice rests with us.

Boulders on the shore of Bubble Pond at Acadia National Park are remnants of glacial moraines.

PLACES OF NOTE

These lists are adapted from *Coast Links,* available from the Maine Coastal Program.

Historical Sites Along the Coast
Colonial Pemaquid (Fort William Henry) Bristol
Eagle Island, South Hapswell
Fort Edgecomb, North Edgecomb
Fort George, Castine
John Paul Jones, Kittery
Fort Knox, Prospect
Fort McClary, Kittery Point
Montpelier, Thomaston
Fort O'Brien (Fort Machias), Machiasport
Fort Popham, Popham Beach

State Parks Along the Coast
Camden Hills, 5,475 acres
Cobscook Bay, Dennysville, 888 acres
Crescent Beach, Cape Elizabeth, 243 acres
Ferry Beach, Saco, 117 acres
Fort Point, Stockton Springs, 154 acres
Lamoine, Lamoine, 55 acres
Moose Point, Searsport, 183 acres
Popham Beach, Phippsburg, 529 acres
Quoddy Head, Lubec, 481 acres
Reid, Georgetown, 766 acres
Scarborough Beach, Scarborough, 5 acres
Two Lights, Cape Elizabeth, 40 acres
Warren Island, Islesboro, 70 acres
Wolf Neck Woods, Freeport, 233 acres

Lighthouses (Dates refer to original construction date and subsequent reconstruction)
Baker Island Light, Cranberry Isles (1828/1855)
Bass Harbor Head Light, Tremont (1858)
Bear Island Light, Cranberry Isles (1839/1889)
Boon Island Light, York (1811/1855)
Burnt Island Light, Southport (1821)

Cape Elizabeth Light, Cape Elizabeth (1829/1874)
Cape Neddick Light, York (1879)
The Cuckolds, Southport (1892/1907)
Dice Head Light, Castine (1829/1937)
Egg Rock Light, Winter Harbor (1875)
Franklin Island Light, Friendship (1805/1855)
Great Duck Island Light, Frenchboro (1890)
Grindle Point Light, Isleboro (1850/1875)
Halfway Rock Light, Portland (1871)
Hendricks Head Light, Southport (1825/1875)
Isle au Haut, Isle au Haut (1907)
Libby Island Light, Machiasport (1817)
Marshal Point Light, St. George (1823/1858)
Matinicus Rock Light, Criehaven (1848)
Monhegan Island Light, Monhegan Plantation (1850)
Moose Peak Light, Jonesport (1827)
Mount Desert Rock Light, 20 Miles off Mt. Desert Island
Nash Island Light, Addison (1838/1873)
Owls Head Light, Owls Head (1826)
Pemaquid Point Light, Bristol (1827)
Petit Manan Light, Milbridge (1817/1855)
Portland Head Light, Cape Elizabeth (1791)
Ram Island Light, Boothbay (1883)
Rockland Breakwater Light, Rockland (1888/1902)
Saddleback Ledge Light, Vinalhaven (1839)
Seguin Light, Georgetown (1795/1887)
Spring Point Ledge Light, South Portland (1897)
Squirrel Point Light, Arrowsic (1898)
Two Bush Island Light, Two Bush Island (1817)
West Quoddy Head, Lubec (1807/1852)
Whitehead Light, St. George (1807/1857)
Wood Island Light, Biddeford (1808/1858)

Fog enshrouds the Portland Head Lighthouse near Portland.

Sunset at Bass Harbor.

FOR MORE INFORMATION

Acadia National Park
Box 177
Bar Harbor, ME 04609

Petit Manan National Wildlife Refuge
P.O. Box 279
Millbridge, ME 04658

Rachel Carson National Wildlife Refuge
RR 2 , Box 751
Wells, ME 04090

Maine Dept. of Inland Fisheries and Wildlife
Station 41, 284 State St.
Augusta, ME 04333

Maine Dept. of Marine Resources
State House Station 21
Augusta , ME 04333

Maine Dept of Conservation
Station 22
Augusta, ME 04333

Maine Critical Areas Program
Maine State Planning Office
184 State St., Station 38
Augusta, ME 04333

Maine Coastal Program
Maine State Planning Office
Statehouse Station 38
184 State St.
Augusta, ME 04333

The Maine Chapter—Nature Conservancy
Box 338, 122 Main St.
Topsham, ME 04086

Maine Coast Heritage Trust
167 Park Row
Brunswick, ME 04011

Maine Audubon Society
118 U.S. Route One,
Gilsland Farm
Falmouth, ME 04105